50 Sweet Treat Recipes for Home

By: Kelly Johnson

Table of Contents

- Classic Chocolate Chip Cookies
- Fudgy Brownies
- Vanilla Bean Cupcakes
- Lemon Bars
- Red Velvet Cake
- Oatmeal Raisin Cookies
- Peanut Butter Blossoms
- Raspberry Swirl Cheesecake
- Blueberry Muffins
- Carrot Cake with Cream Cheese Frosting
- Apple Pie
- Chocolate Fudge
- Snickerdoodle Cookies
- Banana Bread
- Key Lime Pie
- Strawberry Shortcake
- Coconut Macaroons
- Coffee Cake
- Cinnamon Rolls
- S'mores Bars
- Pistachio Almond Biscotti
- Pineapple Upside-Down Cake
- Black Forest Cake
- Pecan Pie
- Chocolate Truffles
- Tiramisu
- Funfetti Sugar Cookies
- Salted Caramel Brownies
- Peanut Butter Cupcakes
- Mocha Chocolate Chip Cookies
- Cherry Pie
- Almond Joy Bars
- Lemon Meringue Pie
- Chocolate Covered Strawberries
- Mint Chocolate Chip Ice Cream

- Peach Cobbler
- Nutella Swirl Pound Cake
- White Chocolate Raspberry Cheesecake
- Apple Crisp
- Caramel Popcorn
- Pumpkin Pie
- Gingerbread Cookies
- Cranberry Orange Bread
- Rice Krispie Treats
- Marble Cake
- Baked Alaska
- Raspberry Chocolate Tart
- Eclairs
- Orange Creamsicle Popsicles
- Chocolate Lava Cake

Classic Chocolate Chip Cookies

Ingredients:

- 1 cup (2 sticks) unsalted butter, softened
- 3/4 cup granulated sugar
- 3/4 cup packed light brown sugar
- 2 large eggs
- 1 teaspoon vanilla extract
- 2 1/4 cups all-purpose flour
- 1 teaspoon baking soda
- 1/2 teaspoon salt
- 2 cups semisweet chocolate chips

Instructions:

1. Preheat your oven to 375°F (190°C). Line baking sheets with parchment paper or silicone baking mats.
2. In a large mixing bowl, cream together the softened butter, granulated sugar, and brown sugar until light and fluffy.
3. Beat in the eggs, one at a time, then stir in the vanilla extract.
4. In a separate bowl, whisk together the flour, baking soda, and salt.
5. Gradually add the dry ingredients to the wet ingredients, mixing until just combined.
6. Fold in the chocolate chips until evenly distributed throughout the dough.
7. Using a cookie scoop or spoon, drop rounded tablespoons of dough onto the prepared baking sheets, spacing them about 2 inches apart.
8. Bake in the preheated oven for 8 to 10 minutes, or until the edges are lightly golden brown.
9. Allow the cookies to cool on the baking sheets for a few minutes before transferring them to wire racks to cool completely.
10. Enjoy your classic chocolate chip cookies with a glass of cold milk or a cup of hot coffee!

Feel free to adjust the baking time to achieve your desired level of chewiness or crispiness in the cookies. And don't forget to share with friends and family—they're sure to love these timeless treats!

Fudgy Brownies

Ingredients:

- 1 cup (2 sticks) unsalted butter
- 2 cups granulated sugar
- 4 large eggs
- 1 teaspoon vanilla extract
- 1 cup all-purpose flour
- 3/4 cup unsweetened cocoa powder
- 1/2 teaspoon salt
- 1 cup semisweet chocolate chips or chunks

Instructions:

1. Preheat your oven to 350°F (175°C). Grease a 9x13-inch baking pan or line it with parchment paper, leaving some overhang on the sides for easy removal.
2. In a medium saucepan, melt the butter over low heat. Once melted, remove from heat and stir in the granulated sugar until well combined. Let it cool slightly.
3. In a large mixing bowl, beat the eggs and vanilla extract together until well blended.
4. Slowly pour the melted butter and sugar mixture into the egg mixture, stirring constantly until smooth.
5. In a separate bowl, sift together the flour, cocoa powder, and salt.
6. Gradually add the dry ingredients to the wet ingredients, mixing until just combined. Be careful not to overmix.
7. Fold in the chocolate chips or chunks until evenly distributed throughout the batter.
8. Pour the batter into the prepared baking pan and spread it out evenly with a spatula.
9. Bake in the preheated oven for 25 to 30 minutes, or until a toothpick inserted into the center comes out with a few moist crumbs clinging to it.
10. Allow the brownies to cool completely in the pan on a wire rack before cutting into squares.
11. Serve and enjoy these decadent fudgy brownies on their own or with a scoop of vanilla ice cream for an extra special treat!

Feel free to adjust the baking time if you prefer your brownies more or less fudgy. And remember, they're best enjoyed fresh but can be stored in an airtight container at room temperature for a few days.

Vanilla Bean Cupcakes

Ingredients:

For the cupcakes:

- 1 1/2 cups all-purpose flour
- 1 1/2 teaspoons baking powder
- 1/4 teaspoon salt
- 1/2 cup (1 stick) unsalted butter, softened
- 1 cup granulated sugar
- 2 large eggs, room temperature
- 1 vanilla bean
- 1 teaspoon vanilla extract
- 1/2 cup whole milk, room temperature

For the vanilla bean frosting:

- 1/2 cup (1 stick) unsalted butter, softened
- 2 cups powdered sugar
- 1 vanilla bean
- 1 teaspoon vanilla extract
- 2-3 tablespoons heavy cream or milk

Instructions:

For the cupcakes:

1. Preheat your oven to 350°F (175°C). Line a muffin tin with cupcake liners.
2. In a medium bowl, whisk together the flour, baking powder, and salt. Set aside.
3. In a large mixing bowl, cream together the softened butter and granulated sugar until light and fluffy.
4. Split the vanilla bean lengthwise and scrape out the seeds using the back of a knife.
5. Add the vanilla bean seeds and vanilla extract to the butter and sugar mixture, and beat until well combined.
6. Add the eggs, one at a time, beating well after each addition.

7. Gradually add the dry ingredients to the wet ingredients, alternating with the milk, beginning and ending with the dry ingredients. Mix until just combined.
8. Divide the batter evenly among the prepared cupcake liners, filling each about 2/3 full.
9. Bake in the preheated oven for 18 to 20 minutes, or until a toothpick inserted into the center comes out clean.
10. Remove the cupcakes from the oven and allow them to cool in the pan for a few minutes before transferring them to a wire rack to cool completely.

For the vanilla bean frosting:

1. In a large mixing bowl, beat the softened butter until smooth and creamy.
2. Split the vanilla bean lengthwise and scrape out the seeds using the back of a knife.
3. Add the vanilla bean seeds and vanilla extract to the butter and beat until well combined.
4. Gradually add the powdered sugar, one cup at a time, beating well after each addition.
5. Add the heavy cream or milk, one tablespoon at a time, until the frosting reaches your desired consistency.
6. Once the cupcakes are completely cooled, frost them with the vanilla bean frosting using a piping bag or offset spatula.
7. Serve and enjoy these delicious vanilla bean cupcakes as a delightful treat for any occasion!

Feel free to garnish the cupcakes with additional vanilla bean seeds or sprinkles for added decoration. These cupcakes are sure to impress with their rich vanilla flavor and tender crumb.

Lemon Bars

Ingredients:

For the crust:

- 1 cup all-purpose flour
- 1/4 cup powdered sugar
- 1/2 cup (1 stick) unsalted butter, cold and cubed

For the lemon filling:

- 1 1/2 cups granulated sugar
- 1/4 cup all-purpose flour
- 4 large eggs
- 2/3 cup freshly squeezed lemon juice (about 3-4 lemons)
- Zest of 2 lemons
- Powdered sugar, for dusting

Instructions:

1. Preheat your oven to 350°F (175°C). Grease or line an 8x8-inch baking pan with parchment paper, leaving some overhang on the sides for easy removal.
2. In a medium mixing bowl, whisk together the flour and powdered sugar for the crust. Add the cold cubed butter and using a pastry cutter or fork, cut the butter into the flour mixture until it resembles coarse crumbs and starts to come together.
3. Press the crust mixture evenly into the bottom of the prepared baking pan. Bake in the preheated oven for 15-18 minutes, or until lightly golden brown.
4. While the crust is baking, prepare the lemon filling. In a separate mixing bowl, whisk together the granulated sugar and flour. Add the eggs, lemon juice, and lemon zest, and whisk until well combined and smooth.
5. Once the crust is baked, remove it from the oven and pour the lemon filling over the hot crust.
6. Return the pan to the oven and bake for an additional 20-25 minutes, or until the filling is set and no longer jiggles when gently shaken.

7. Remove the lemon bars from the oven and allow them to cool completely in the pan on a wire rack.
8. Once cooled, dust the top of the lemon bars with powdered sugar. Use the parchment paper overhang to lift the bars out of the pan and onto a cutting board. Cut into squares or rectangles.
9. Serve and enjoy these refreshing lemon bars as a delicious dessert or snack!

Store any leftover lemon bars in an airtight container in the refrigerator for up to 3-4 days. The tangy lemon flavor and buttery crust make these bars a perfect treat for any occasion.

Red Velvet Cake

Ingredients:

For the cake:

- 2 1/2 cups all-purpose flour
- 1 1/2 cups granulated sugar
- 1 teaspoon baking soda
- 1 teaspoon cocoa powder
- 1 teaspoon salt
- 2 large eggs
- 1 1/2 cups vegetable oil
- 1 cup buttermilk, room temperature
- 2 tablespoons red food coloring
- 1 teaspoon white vinegar
- 1 teaspoon vanilla extract

For the cream cheese frosting:

- 16 ounces cream cheese, softened
- 1/2 cup (1 stick) unsalted butter, softened
- 4 cups powdered sugar
- 1 teaspoon vanilla extract

Instructions:

For the cake:

1. Preheat your oven to 350°F (175°C). Grease and flour two 9-inch round cake pans or line them with parchment paper.
2. In a large mixing bowl, sift together the flour, sugar, baking soda, cocoa powder, and salt.
3. In another bowl, beat the eggs, vegetable oil, buttermilk, red food coloring, vinegar, and vanilla extract until well combined.

4. Gradually add the wet ingredients to the dry ingredients, mixing until smooth and well incorporated.
5. Divide the batter evenly between the prepared cake pans.
6. Bake in the preheated oven for 25-30 minutes, or until a toothpick inserted into the center comes out clean.
7. Remove the cakes from the oven and let them cool in the pans for 10 minutes before transferring them to wire racks to cool completely.

For the cream cheese frosting:

1. In a large mixing bowl, beat the cream cheese and butter until smooth and creamy.
2. Gradually add the powdered sugar, one cup at a time, beating well after each addition.
3. Add the vanilla extract and beat until the frosting is smooth and creamy.

To assemble:

1. Once the cakes are completely cooled, place one layer on a serving plate or cake stand.
2. Spread a layer of cream cheese frosting evenly over the top of the first layer.
3. Place the second layer on top and frost the top and sides of the cake with the remaining frosting.
4. If desired, decorate the cake with cake crumbs or red velvet cake crumbs for added texture.
5. Slice and serve the red velvet cake, and enjoy this classic dessert with friends and family!

Store any leftover cake in an airtight container in the refrigerator for up to 3-4 days. The moist, velvety texture and creamy frosting make this red velvet cake a crowd-pleasing favorite for any occasion.

Oatmeal Raisin Cookies

Ingredients:

- 1 cup (2 sticks) unsalted butter, softened
- 1 cup packed light brown sugar
- 1/2 cup granulated sugar
- 2 large eggs
- 1 teaspoon vanilla extract
- 1 1/2 cups all-purpose flour
- 1 teaspoon baking soda
- 1 teaspoon ground cinnamon
- 1/2 teaspoon salt
- 3 cups old-fashioned rolled oats
- 1 cup raisins

Instructions:

1. Preheat your oven to 350°F (175°C). Line baking sheets with parchment paper or silicone baking mats.
2. In a large mixing bowl, cream together the softened butter, brown sugar, and granulated sugar until light and fluffy.
3. Beat in the eggs, one at a time, then stir in the vanilla extract.
4. In a separate bowl, whisk together the flour, baking soda, cinnamon, and salt.
5. Gradually add the dry ingredients to the wet ingredients, mixing until just combined.
6. Stir in the rolled oats and raisins until evenly distributed throughout the dough.
7. Using a cookie scoop or spoon, drop rounded tablespoons of dough onto the prepared baking sheets, spacing them about 2 inches apart.
8. Gently flatten each dough ball with the palm of your hand or the back of a spoon.
9. Bake in the preheated oven for 10 to 12 minutes, or until the edges are lightly golden brown.
10. Allow the cookies to cool on the baking sheets for a few minutes before transferring them to wire racks to cool completely.
11. Once cooled, store the oatmeal raisin cookies in an airtight container at room temperature for up to one week.
12. Enjoy these delicious oatmeal raisin cookies as a tasty snack or dessert!

Feel free to customize the cookies by adding chopped nuts or chocolate chips if desired. These cookies are soft, chewy, and filled with wholesome oats and sweet raisins, making them a beloved classic for cookie lovers of all ages.

Peanut Butter Blossoms

Ingredients:

- 1/2 cup (1 stick) unsalted butter, softened
- 3/4 cup creamy peanut butter
- 1/3 cup granulated sugar
- 1/3 cup packed light brown sugar
- 1 large egg
- 1 teaspoon vanilla extract
- 1 1/2 cups all-purpose flour
- 1 teaspoon baking soda
- 1/2 teaspoon salt
- About 24 chocolate Hershey's Kisses, unwrapped
- Additional granulated sugar for rolling

Instructions:

1. Preheat your oven to 375°F (190°C). Line baking sheets with parchment paper or silicone baking mats.
2. In a large mixing bowl, cream together the softened butter, peanut butter, granulated sugar, and brown sugar until light and fluffy.
3. Beat in the egg and vanilla extract until well combined.
4. In a separate bowl, whisk together the flour, baking soda, and salt.
5. Gradually add the dry ingredients to the wet ingredients, mixing until just combined.
6. Shape the dough into 1-inch balls. Roll each ball in granulated sugar until coated.
7. Place the sugared dough balls onto the prepared baking sheets, spacing them about 2 inches apart.
8. Bake in the preheated oven for 8 to 10 minutes, or until the edges are lightly golden brown.
9. Remove the baking sheets from the oven and immediately press a chocolate Hershey's Kiss into the center of each cookie, pressing down gently until the edges crack slightly.
10. Allow the cookies to cool on the baking sheets for a few minutes before transferring them to wire racks to cool completely.

11. Once cooled, store the Peanut Butter Blossoms in an airtight container at room temperature for up to one week.
12. Enjoy these delicious Peanut Butter Blossoms as a classic cookie treat that's perfect for any occasion!

Feel free to customize these cookies by using different types of Hershey's Kisses or adding a sprinkle of sea salt on top for a sweet and salty twist. These cookies are sure to be a hit with peanut butter and chocolate lovers alike!

Raspberry Swirl Cheesecake

Ingredients:

For the crust:

- 1 1/2 cups graham cracker crumbs
- 1/4 cup granulated sugar
- 1/2 cup (1 stick) unsalted butter, melted

For the raspberry swirl:

- 1 1/2 cups fresh or frozen raspberries
- 1/4 cup granulated sugar
- 1 tablespoon lemon juice

For the cheesecake filling:

- 24 ounces cream cheese, softened
- 1 cup granulated sugar
- 1 teaspoon vanilla extract
- 4 large eggs
- 1/2 cup sour cream
- 1/4 cup all-purpose flour

Instructions:

1. Preheat your oven to 325°F (160°C). Grease a 9-inch springform pan and line the bottom with parchment paper.
2. In a medium bowl, mix together the graham cracker crumbs, granulated sugar, and melted butter until well combined. Press the mixture evenly into the bottom of the prepared springform pan.
3. In a small saucepan, combine the raspberries, granulated sugar, and lemon juice. Cook over medium heat, stirring occasionally, until the raspberries break down

and the mixture thickens, about 5-7 minutes. Remove from heat and strain the mixture through a fine mesh sieve to remove the seeds. Set aside to cool.
4. In a large mixing bowl, beat the cream cheese, granulated sugar, and vanilla extract until smooth and creamy.
5. Add the eggs one at a time, beating well after each addition. Add the sour cream and flour, and mix until smooth and well combined.
6. Pour the cheesecake filling over the prepared crust in the springform pan.
7. Drop spoonfuls of the raspberry sauce on top of the cheesecake filling. Use a knife or toothpick to gently swirl the raspberry sauce into the cheesecake batter to create a marbled effect.
8. Place the springform pan on a baking sheet and bake in the preheated oven for 55-60 minutes, or until the edges are set and the center is slightly jiggly.
9. Turn off the oven and leave the cheesecake in the oven with the door slightly ajar for about 1 hour to cool gradually.
10. Remove the cheesecake from the oven and let it cool completely at room temperature. Then, refrigerate the cheesecake for at least 4 hours, or preferably overnight, to chill and set.
11. Once chilled, carefully remove the sides of the springform pan and transfer the cheesecake to a serving plate.
12. Slice and serve the raspberry swirl cheesecake, and enjoy this decadent dessert with its creamy texture and tangy raspberry flavor!

Store any leftovers in the refrigerator for up to 5 days. This Raspberry Swirl Cheesecake is perfect for special occasions or any time you want to indulge in a luxurious dessert.

Blueberry Muffins

Ingredients:

- 2 cups all-purpose flour
- 1/2 cup granulated sugar
- 1 tablespoon baking powder
- 1/2 teaspoon salt
- 1/2 cup (1 stick) unsalted butter, melted and cooled
- 2 large eggs
- 1 cup milk
- 1 teaspoon vanilla extract
- 1 1/2 cups fresh or frozen blueberries (if using frozen, do not thaw)

Instructions:

1. Preheat your oven to 375°F (190°C). Line a muffin tin with paper liners or grease the cups with non-stick cooking spray.
2. In a large mixing bowl, whisk together the flour, sugar, baking powder, and salt until well combined.
3. In a separate bowl, beat the melted butter, eggs, milk, and vanilla extract until well combined.
4. Pour the wet ingredients into the dry ingredients and stir until just combined. Do not overmix; the batter should be lumpy.
5. Gently fold in the blueberries until evenly distributed throughout the batter.
6. Divide the batter evenly among the prepared muffin cups, filling each about 2/3 full.
7. Optional: sprinkle a little granulated sugar on top of each muffin before baking for a slightly crunchy topping.
8. Bake in the preheated oven for 18-20 minutes, or until the tops are golden brown and a toothpick inserted into the center of a muffin comes out clean.
9. Remove the muffins from the oven and let them cool in the tin for a few minutes before transferring them to a wire rack to cool completely.
10. Serve the blueberry muffins warm or at room temperature, and enjoy their tender texture and burst of juicy blueberries!

These blueberry muffins are perfect for breakfast on the go, a midday snack, or a sweet treat any time of day. Store any leftovers in an airtight container at room temperature for up to 3 days, or freeze for longer storage.

Carrot Cake with Cream Cheese Frosting

Ingredients:

For the carrot cake:

- 2 cups all-purpose flour
- 2 teaspoons baking powder
- 1 1/2 teaspoons baking soda
- 1/2 teaspoon salt
- 2 teaspoons ground cinnamon
- 1/2 teaspoon ground nutmeg
- 1 cup granulated sugar
- 1 cup packed light brown sugar
- 1 cup vegetable oil
- 4 large eggs
- 2 teaspoons vanilla extract
- 3 cups grated carrots (about 3-4 medium carrots)
- 1 cup chopped walnuts or pecans (optional)
- 1/2 cup shredded coconut (optional)

For the cream cheese frosting:

- 8 ounces cream cheese, softened
- 1/2 cup (1 stick) unsalted butter, softened
- 4 cups powdered sugar
- 1 teaspoon vanilla extract

Instructions:

For the carrot cake:

1. Preheat your oven to 350°F (175°C). Grease and flour two 9-inch round cake pans or line them with parchment paper.
2. In a medium bowl, whisk together the flour, baking powder, baking soda, salt, cinnamon, and nutmeg until well combined.
3. In a large mixing bowl, whisk together the granulated sugar, brown sugar, vegetable oil, eggs, and vanilla extract until smooth.

4. Gradually add the dry ingredients to the wet ingredients, mixing until just combined.
5. Fold in the grated carrots, chopped nuts (if using), and shredded coconut (if using) until evenly distributed throughout the batter.
6. Divide the batter evenly between the prepared cake pans, spreading it out evenly with a spatula.
7. Bake in the preheated oven for 25-30 minutes, or until a toothpick inserted into the center of the cakes comes out clean.
8. Remove the cakes from the oven and let them cool in the pans for 10 minutes before transferring them to wire racks to cool completely.

For the cream cheese frosting:

1. In a large mixing bowl, beat the softened cream cheese and butter together until smooth and creamy.
2. Gradually add the powdered sugar, one cup at a time, beating well after each addition.
3. Add the vanilla extract and beat until the frosting is smooth and creamy.

To assemble:

1. Once the cakes are completely cooled, place one layer on a serving plate or cake stand.
2. Spread a layer of cream cheese frosting evenly over the top of the first layer.
3. Place the second layer on top and frost the top and sides of the cake with the remaining frosting.
4. If desired, decorate the cake with additional grated carrots or chopped nuts.
5. Slice and serve the carrot cake, and enjoy this classic dessert with its moist, flavorful crumb and creamy frosting!

Store any leftovers in the refrigerator for up to 5 days. This carrot cake with cream cheese frosting is perfect for any celebration or gathering, or simply as a special treat for yourself!

Apple Pie

Ingredients:

For the crust:

- 2 1/2 cups all-purpose flour
- 1 teaspoon salt
- 1 tablespoon granulated sugar
- 1 cup (2 sticks) unsalted butter, cold and cut into cubes
- 1/4 to 1/2 cup ice water

For the filling:

- 6-7 large apples (such as Granny Smith, Honeycrisp, or a mix), peeled, cored, and thinly sliced
- 3/4 cup granulated sugar
- 2 tablespoons all-purpose flour
- 1 teaspoon ground cinnamon
- 1/4 teaspoon ground nutmeg
- 1 tablespoon lemon juice
- 1 tablespoon unsalted butter, cut into small pieces

For assembly:

- 1 egg, beaten (for egg wash)
- 1 tablespoon granulated sugar (for sprinkling)

Instructions:

1. To make the crust, in a large mixing bowl, whisk together the flour, salt, and sugar. Add the cold cubed butter and use a pastry cutter or your fingers to work the butter into the flour mixture until it resembles coarse crumbs.

2. Gradually add the ice water, 1 tablespoon at a time, mixing with a fork until the dough just begins to come together. Be careful not to overwork the dough. If the dough holds together when pinched, it's ready.
3. Divide the dough into two equal portions, shape each into a disk, and wrap them tightly in plastic wrap. Chill the dough in the refrigerator for at least 1 hour, or overnight.
4. Preheat your oven to 375°F (190°C). On a lightly floured surface, roll out one disk of dough into a circle about 12 inches in diameter. Carefully transfer the rolled-out dough to a 9-inch pie dish, gently pressing it into the bottom and up the sides.
5. In a large mixing bowl, combine the sliced apples, granulated sugar, flour, cinnamon, nutmeg, and lemon juice. Toss until the apples are evenly coated.
6. Pour the apple filling into the prepared pie crust, spreading it out evenly. Dot the top of the filling with small pieces of butter.
7. Roll out the second disk of dough into a circle about 12 inches in diameter. Carefully place it over the filling. Trim any excess dough, leaving about a 1-inch overhang. Fold the overhang under itself and crimp the edges to seal.
8. Use a sharp knife to make several small slits in the top crust to allow steam to escape during baking. Alternatively, you can make a decorative lattice crust.
9. Brush the top crust with the beaten egg and sprinkle with granulated sugar.
10. Place the pie on a baking sheet to catch any drips, and bake in the preheated oven for 45 to 55 minutes, or until the crust is golden brown and the filling is bubbling.
11. If the crust starts to brown too quickly, you can cover the edges with foil halfway through baking to prevent over-browning.
12. Remove the pie from the oven and let it cool on a wire rack for at least 2 hours before slicing and serving.
13. Serve the apple pie warm or at room temperature, optionally with a scoop of vanilla ice cream or a dollop of whipped cream.
14. Enjoy this classic apple pie with its tender, spiced apple filling and buttery flaky crust!

Store any leftovers covered at room temperature for up to 2 days, or in the refrigerator for up to 5 days. The pie can also be frozen for longer storage—just wrap it tightly in plastic wrap and foil before freezing.

Chocolate Fudge

Ingredients:

- 3 cups semisweet chocolate chips
- 1 (14-ounce) can sweetened condensed milk
- 1/4 cup unsalted butter
- 1 teaspoon vanilla extract
- Optional toppings: chopped nuts, sprinkles, sea salt

Instructions:

1. Line an 8x8-inch square baking dish with parchment paper, leaving some overhang on the sides for easy removal later. Lightly grease the parchment paper with butter or non-stick cooking spray.
2. In a medium saucepan, combine the chocolate chips, sweetened condensed milk, and unsalted butter.
3. Cook the mixture over low heat, stirring constantly, until the chocolate chips and butter are melted and the mixture is smooth and well combined. Be careful not to let the mixture scorch.
4. Once the mixture is smooth, remove the saucepan from the heat and stir in the vanilla extract until well incorporated.
5. Pour the melted chocolate mixture into the prepared baking dish, spreading it out evenly with a spatula.
6. If desired, sprinkle your choice of toppings (such as chopped nuts, sprinkles, or sea salt) evenly over the top of the fudge.
7. Place the baking dish in the refrigerator and chill the fudge for at least 2 hours, or until firm.
8. Once the fudge is firm, use the parchment paper overhang to lift it out of the baking dish. Place it on a cutting board and use a sharp knife to cut the fudge into squares or rectangles.
9. Serve and enjoy the chocolate fudge as a delicious homemade treat!

Store any leftover fudge in an airtight container in the refrigerator for up to one week.

The rich and creamy texture of this chocolate fudge makes it irresistible to chocolate lovers of all ages.

Snickerdoodle Cookies

Ingredients:

For the cookie dough:

- 1 cup (2 sticks) unsalted butter, softened
- 1 1/2 cups granulated sugar
- 2 large eggs
- 1 teaspoon vanilla extract
- 2 3/4 cups all-purpose flour
- 2 teaspoons cream of tartar
- 1 teaspoon baking soda
- 1/2 teaspoon salt

For the cinnamon-sugar coating:

- 1/4 cup granulated sugar
- 2 tablespoons ground cinnamon

Instructions:

1. Preheat your oven to 375°F (190°C). Line baking sheets with parchment paper or silicone baking mats.
2. In a large mixing bowl, cream together the softened butter and granulated sugar until light and fluffy.
3. Beat in the eggs, one at a time, then stir in the vanilla extract.
4. In a separate bowl, whisk together the flour, cream of tartar, baking soda, and salt.
5. Gradually add the dry ingredients to the wet ingredients, mixing until just combined.
6. In a small bowl, mix together the granulated sugar and ground cinnamon for the coating.
7. Shape the cookie dough into 1-inch balls (about 1 tablespoon of dough each).
8. Roll each dough ball in the cinnamon-sugar mixture until evenly coated.
9. Place the coated dough balls onto the prepared baking sheets, spacing them about 2 inches apart.

10. Gently flatten each dough ball with the bottom of a glass or the palm of your hand.
11. Bake in the preheated oven for 8 to 10 minutes, or until the edges are set and the tops are slightly cracked.
12. Allow the cookies to cool on the baking sheets for a few minutes before transferring them to wire racks to cool completely.
13. Once cooled, serve and enjoy these delightful snickerdoodle cookies with a glass of milk or a cup of tea!

Store any leftover cookies in an airtight container at room temperature for up to one week. These soft, chewy cookies with their cinnamon-sugar coating are sure to be a hit with family and friends!

Banana Bread

Ingredients:

- 2 to 3 ripe bananas, mashed (about 1 cup)
- 1/3 cup unsalted butter, melted
- 3/4 cup granulated sugar
- 1 large egg, beaten
- 1 teaspoon vanilla extract
- 1 1/2 cups all-purpose flour
- 1 teaspoon baking soda
- 1/2 teaspoon salt
- Optional mix-ins: chopped nuts (such as walnuts or pecans), chocolate chips, dried fruit

Instructions:

1. Preheat your oven to 350°F (175°C). Grease a 9x5-inch loaf pan or line it with parchment paper.
2. In a large mixing bowl, mash the ripe bananas with a fork until smooth.
3. Add the melted butter to the mashed bananas and stir until well combined.
4. Add the granulated sugar, beaten egg, and vanilla extract to the banana mixture, and mix until smooth.
5. In a separate bowl, whisk together the all-purpose flour, baking soda, and salt.
6. Gradually add the dry ingredients to the wet ingredients, stirring until just combined. Be careful not to overmix; the batter should be lumpy.
7. If desired, fold in any optional mix-ins such as chopped nuts, chocolate chips, or dried fruit until evenly distributed throughout the batter.
8. Pour the batter into the prepared loaf pan, spreading it out evenly with a spatula.
9. Bake in the preheated oven for 50 to 60 minutes, or until a toothpick inserted into the center comes out clean.
10. If the top of the bread starts to brown too quickly, you can cover it loosely with aluminum foil halfway through baking.
11. Once baked, remove the banana bread from the oven and let it cool in the pan for 10 minutes before transferring it to a wire rack to cool completely.
12. Slice and serve the banana bread, and enjoy its moist texture and sweet banana flavor!

Store any leftover banana bread in an airtight container at room temperature for up to 3 days, or in the refrigerator for up to one week. You can also freeze sliced banana bread for longer storage—just wrap it tightly in plastic wrap and foil before freezing. Enjoy this classic banana bread recipe for a delicious homemade treat!

Key Lime Pie

Ingredients:

For the crust:

- 1 1/2 cups graham cracker crumbs
- 1/4 cup granulated sugar
- 1/3 cup unsalted butter, melted

For the filling:

- 1 (14-ounce) can sweetened condensed milk
- 4 large egg yolks
- 1/2 cup key lime juice (freshly squeezed if possible)
- 1 tablespoon key lime zest (from about 4-5 key limes)

For the whipped cream topping:

- 1 cup heavy cream
- 2 tablespoons powdered sugar
- 1/2 teaspoon vanilla extract

Instructions:

1. Preheat your oven to 350°F (175°C).
2. In a mixing bowl, combine the graham cracker crumbs, granulated sugar, and melted butter. Mix until the crumbs are evenly moistened.
3. Press the mixture firmly and evenly into the bottom and up the sides of a 9-inch pie dish.
4. Bake the crust in the preheated oven for 10 minutes. Remove from the oven and let it cool while you prepare the filling.
5. In a separate mixing bowl, whisk together the sweetened condensed milk and egg yolks until well combined.

6. Gradually add the key lime juice and key lime zest to the condensed milk mixture, whisking until smooth and thickened.
7. Pour the filling into the cooled graham cracker crust, spreading it out evenly with a spatula.
8. Bake the pie in the preheated oven for 15-18 minutes, or until the filling is set but still slightly jiggly in the center.
9. Remove the pie from the oven and let it cool to room temperature. Then, refrigerate the pie for at least 2 hours, or until well chilled.
10. In a mixing bowl, whip the heavy cream, powdered sugar, and vanilla extract until stiff peaks form.
11. Spread or pipe the whipped cream over the chilled pie.
12. Optionally, garnish the pie with additional key lime zest or slices before serving.
13. Slice and enjoy this refreshing key lime pie as a delightful dessert!

Store any leftover key lime pie in the refrigerator for up to 3 days. Its tangy, creamy filling and buttery graham cracker crust make it a perfect treat for any occasion, especially during warmer months.

Strawberry Shortcake

Ingredients:

For the biscuits:

- 2 cups all-purpose flour
- 1/4 cup granulated sugar
- 1 tablespoon baking powder
- 1/2 teaspoon salt
- 1/2 cup (1 stick) unsalted butter, cold and cut into cubes
- 2/3 cup milk
- 1 teaspoon vanilla extract

For the strawberries:

- 4 cups fresh strawberries, hulled and sliced
- 1/4 cup granulated sugar
- 1 tablespoon lemon juice

For the whipped cream:

- 1 cup heavy cream
- 2 tablespoons powdered sugar
- 1/2 teaspoon vanilla extract

Instructions:

For the biscuits:

1. Preheat your oven to 425°F (220°C). Line a baking sheet with parchment paper.
2. In a large mixing bowl, whisk together the flour, sugar, baking powder, and salt.
3. Add the cold cubed butter to the flour mixture. Using a pastry cutter or your fingers, cut the butter into the flour until the mixture resembles coarse crumbs.
4. In a separate bowl, mix together the milk and vanilla extract.
5. Gradually add the milk mixture to the flour mixture, stirring until the dough just comes together. Be careful not to overmix.

6. Turn the dough out onto a lightly floured surface and gently knead it a few times until it forms a smooth ball.
7. Pat the dough into a circle about 1-inch thick. Use a biscuit cutter or the rim of a glass to cut out biscuits. Place the biscuits on the prepared baking sheet.
8. Bake in the preheated oven for 12 to 15 minutes, or until the biscuits are golden brown.
9. Remove the biscuits from the oven and let them cool on a wire rack.

For the strawberries:

1. In a mixing bowl, combine the sliced strawberries, granulated sugar, and lemon juice. Stir until the strawberries are well coated in the sugar mixture.
2. Let the strawberries sit at room temperature for about 15-20 minutes, allowing them to release their juices and become slightly syrupy.

For the whipped cream:

1. In a mixing bowl, whip the heavy cream, powdered sugar, and vanilla extract until stiff peaks form.

To assemble:

1. Split the biscuits in half horizontally.
2. Place a spoonful of strawberries with their juices onto the bottom half of each biscuit.
3. Top the strawberries with a dollop of whipped cream.
4. Place the other half of the biscuit on top.
5. Optionally, garnish each strawberry shortcake with a fresh strawberry or a sprinkle of powdered sugar.
6. Serve immediately and enjoy this classic strawberry shortcake as a delightful dessert!

Strawberry shortcake is best enjoyed fresh, but you can store any leftovers in the refrigerator for up to one day. The combination of sweet strawberries, fluffy biscuits, and creamy whipped cream makes it a perfect summer treat.

Coconut Macaroons

Ingredients:

- 3 cups sweetened shredded coconut
- 2/3 cup sweetened condensed milk
- 2 large egg whites
- 1 teaspoon vanilla extract
- 1/4 teaspoon salt

Instructions:

1. Preheat your oven to 325°F (160°C). Line a baking sheet with parchment paper or a silicone baking mat.
2. In a large mixing bowl, combine the sweetened shredded coconut, sweetened condensed milk, vanilla extract, and salt. Stir until well combined.
3. In a separate mixing bowl, beat the egg whites until stiff peaks form.
4. Gently fold the beaten egg whites into the coconut mixture until evenly incorporated. Be careful not to deflate the egg whites too much.
5. Using a spoon or cookie scoop, drop rounded tablespoons of the coconut mixture onto the prepared baking sheet, spacing them about 1 inch apart.
6. If desired, you can shape the coconut mixture into mounds or use your fingers to shape them into nests.
7. Bake in the preheated oven for 15 to 20 minutes, or until the edges of the macaroons are golden brown.
8. Remove the baking sheet from the oven and let the macaroons cool on the baking sheet for a few minutes before transferring them to a wire rack to cool completely.
9. Once cooled, you can optionally drizzle melted chocolate over the macaroons or dip the bottoms of the macaroons in melted chocolate for added flavor.
10. Let the chocolate set before serving or storing the macaroons.
11. Serve and enjoy these delicious coconut macaroons as a sweet treat or dessert!

Store any leftover coconut macaroons in an airtight container at room temperature for up to one week. These chewy, coconutty cookies are perfect for any occasion and are sure to be a hit with coconut lovers!

Coffee Cake

Ingredients:

For the cake:

- 2 cups all-purpose flour
- 1 cup granulated sugar
- 1/2 cup unsalted butter, softened
- 1 cup sour cream
- 2 large eggs
- 1 teaspoon vanilla extract
- 1 teaspoon baking powder
- 1/2 teaspoon baking soda
- 1/4 teaspoon salt

For the streusel topping:

- 1/2 cup all-purpose flour
- 1/2 cup granulated sugar
- 1/4 cup unsalted butter, softened
- 1 teaspoon ground cinnamon

Instructions:

1. Preheat your oven to 350°F (175°C). Grease and flour a 9x9-inch baking pan or line it with parchment paper.
2. In a medium mixing bowl, prepare the streusel topping by combining the flour, sugar, softened butter, and ground cinnamon. Mix with a fork or your fingers until crumbly. Set aside.
3. In a large mixing bowl, cream together the softened butter and granulated sugar until light and fluffy.
4. Add the eggs, one at a time, beating well after each addition. Stir in the vanilla extract.
5. In a separate bowl, whisk together the flour, baking powder, baking soda, and salt.
6. Gradually add the dry ingredients to the wet ingredients, alternating with the sour cream, beginning and ending with the dry ingredients. Mix until just combined.

7. Spread half of the cake batter into the prepared baking pan, smoothing it out with a spatula.
8. Sprinkle half of the streusel topping evenly over the batter in the pan.
9. Spoon the remaining cake batter over the streusel topping and spread it out evenly.
10. Sprinkle the remaining streusel topping over the top of the cake batter.
11. Bake in the preheated oven for 35 to 40 minutes, or until a toothpick inserted into the center comes out clean.
12. Remove the coffee cake from the oven and let it cool in the pan for about 10 minutes before transferring it to a wire rack to cool completely.
13. Once cooled, slice and serve the coffee cake, and enjoy it as a delightful breakfast or snack!

Store any leftover coffee cake in an airtight container at room temperature for up to 3 days. This classic coffee cake is sure to become a favorite in your household with its moist texture and delicious streusel topping.

Cinnamon Rolls

Ingredients:

For the dough:

- 1 cup warm milk (110°F-115°F)
- 2 1/4 teaspoons active dry yeast (1 packet)
- 1/2 cup granulated sugar
- 1/3 cup unsalted butter, melted
- 2 large eggs, room temperature
- 4 1/2 to 5 cups all-purpose flour
- 1 teaspoon salt

For the filling:

- 1/3 cup unsalted butter, softened
- 1 cup packed brown sugar
- 2 tablespoons ground cinnamon

For the glaze:

- 1 cup powdered sugar
- 1-2 tablespoons milk or cream
- 1/2 teaspoon vanilla extract

Instructions:

1. In a small bowl, dissolve the active dry yeast in the warm milk. Let it sit for 5-10 minutes until foamy.
2. In a large mixing bowl or the bowl of a stand mixer fitted with the dough hook attachment, combine the dissolved yeast mixture, sugar, melted butter, eggs, 4 1/2 cups of flour, and salt. Mix until well combined.

3. Knead the dough for about 5-7 minutes, adding additional flour as needed, until the dough is smooth and elastic. It should be slightly tacky but not sticky.
4. Place the dough in a greased bowl, cover with a clean kitchen towel or plastic wrap, and let it rise in a warm place for about 1 to 1 1/2 hours, or until doubled in size.
5. While the dough is rising, prepare the filling by mixing together the softened butter, brown sugar, and ground cinnamon until well combined. Set aside.
6. Once the dough has doubled in size, punch it down to release the air. Transfer it to a lightly floured surface and roll it out into a rectangle, about 16x20 inches in size.
7. Spread the cinnamon sugar filling evenly over the rolled-out dough, leaving a small border around the edges.
8. Starting from one long edge, tightly roll up the dough into a log. Pinch the seam to seal.
9. Use a sharp knife or dental floss to cut the rolled dough into 12 equal-sized pieces.
10. Place the cinnamon rolls in a greased 9x13-inch baking pan, leaving a little space between each roll. Cover the pan with a kitchen towel and let the rolls rise for an additional 30-45 minutes, until puffed up.
11. Preheat your oven to 350°F (175°C). Once the rolls have risen, bake them in the preheated oven for 25-30 minutes, or until golden brown.
12. While the cinnamon rolls are baking, prepare the glaze by whisking together the powdered sugar, milk or cream, and vanilla extract until smooth. Adjust the consistency by adding more milk or powdered sugar as needed.
13. Once the cinnamon rolls are done baking, remove them from the oven and let them cool in the pan for a few minutes.
14. Drizzle the glaze over the warm cinnamon rolls and serve immediately.

Enjoy these homemade cinnamon rolls warm, with a cup of coffee or tea, for a delicious breakfast or brunch treat!

S'mores Bars

Ingredients:

- 2 cups graham cracker crumbs (about 12-14 graham crackers)
- 1/2 cup unsalted butter, melted
- 1/4 cup granulated sugar
- 1/2 teaspoon salt
- 2 cups milk chocolate chips or chopped chocolate
- 2 1/2 cups mini marshmallows

Instructions:

1. Preheat your oven to 350°F (175°C). Grease a 9x9-inch baking pan or line it with parchment paper, leaving some overhang on the sides for easy removal.
2. In a mixing bowl, combine the graham cracker crumbs, melted butter, granulated sugar, and salt. Stir until the mixture resembles coarse crumbs and is well combined.
3. Press the graham cracker mixture firmly and evenly into the bottom of the prepared baking pan.
4. Bake the crust in the preheated oven for 8-10 minutes, or until lightly golden brown. Remove from the oven and let it cool slightly.
5. Sprinkle the chocolate chips evenly over the warm crust.
6. Scatter the mini marshmallows evenly over the chocolate chips, pressing them lightly into the chocolate.
7. Return the pan to the oven and bake for an additional 10-12 minutes, or until the marshmallows are puffed and golden brown.
8. Remove the pan from the oven and let it cool completely on a wire rack.
9. Once cooled, use a sharp knife to cut the s'mores bars into squares or rectangles.
10. Serve and enjoy these delicious s'mores bars as a sweet treat or dessert!

These s'mores bars are perfect for satisfying your craving for s'mores any time of year, whether you're indoors or outdoors. They're great for parties, picnics, or simply as a special treat for yourself and your loved ones.

Pistachio Almond Biscotti

Ingredients:

- 2 cups all-purpose flour
- 1 teaspoon baking powder
- 1/4 teaspoon salt
- 1/2 cup unsalted butter, softened
- 3/4 cup granulated sugar
- 2 large eggs
- 1 teaspoon almond extract
- 1/2 cup shelled pistachios, chopped
- 1/2 cup almonds, chopped
- Optional: melted chocolate for dipping

Instructions:

1. Preheat your oven to 350°F (175°C). Line a baking sheet with parchment paper or a silicone baking mat.
2. In a medium mixing bowl, whisk together the flour, baking powder, and salt. Set aside.
3. In a large mixing bowl, cream together the softened butter and granulated sugar until light and fluffy.
4. Beat in the eggs, one at a time, until well combined. Stir in the almond extract.
5. Gradually add the dry ingredients to the wet ingredients, mixing until a dough forms.
6. Fold in the chopped pistachios and almonds until evenly distributed throughout the dough.
7. Divide the dough in half. On a lightly floured surface, shape each half into a log about 12 inches long and 2 inches wide. Place the logs on the prepared baking sheet, spacing them a few inches apart.
8. Bake in the preheated oven for 25-30 minutes, or until the logs are lightly golden brown and firm to the touch.
9. Remove the baking sheet from the oven and let the logs cool for about 10 minutes. Reduce the oven temperature to 325°F (160°C).
10. Using a sharp knife, carefully slice the logs diagonally into 1/2-inch thick slices.

11. Arrange the biscotti cut side down on the baking sheet and bake for an additional 10-15 minutes, or until the biscotti are golden brown and crisp.
12. Remove the biscotti from the oven and let them cool completely on a wire rack.
13. If desired, you can dip the cooled biscotti in melted chocolate and let them set before serving.
14. Serve and enjoy these delicious pistachio almond biscotti with a cup of coffee or tea!

Store any leftover biscotti in an airtight container at room temperature for up to two weeks. These crunchy, nutty cookies are perfect for dunking and make a lovely homemade gift for friends and family.

Pineapple Upside-Down Cake

Ingredients:

For the topping:

- 1/4 cup unsalted butter
- 3/4 cup packed brown sugar
- 7 to 8 pineapple rings (canned or fresh)
- Maraschino cherries, drained

For the cake batter:

- 1 1/2 cups all-purpose flour
- 1 teaspoon baking powder
- 1/4 teaspoon baking soda
- 1/4 teaspoon salt
- 1/2 cup unsalted butter, softened
- 3/4 cup granulated sugar
- 2 large eggs
- 1 teaspoon vanilla extract
- 1/2 cup buttermilk

Instructions:

1. Preheat your oven to 350°F (175°C). Grease a 9-inch round cake pan or line it with parchment paper.
2. In a small saucepan, melt the butter over low heat. Add the brown sugar and stir until dissolved. Pour the mixture into the prepared cake pan, spreading it out evenly.
3. Arrange the pineapple rings on top of the brown sugar mixture in the cake pan. Place a maraschino cherry in the center of each pineapple ring and in between the rings, if desired. Set aside.
4. In a medium mixing bowl, whisk together the flour, baking powder, baking soda, and salt. Set aside.
5. In a large mixing bowl, cream together the softened butter and granulated sugar until light and fluffy.
6. Beat in the eggs, one at a time, until well combined. Stir in the vanilla extract.

7. Gradually add the dry ingredients to the wet ingredients, alternating with the buttermilk, beginning and ending with the dry ingredients. Mix until just combined.
8. Pour the cake batter over the pineapple and brown sugar mixture in the cake pan, spreading it out evenly.
9. Bake in the preheated oven for 35 to 40 minutes, or until a toothpick inserted into the center of the cake comes out clean.
10. Remove the cake from the oven and let it cool in the pan for 5 minutes.
11. Place a serving plate upside down over the cake pan. Carefully invert the cake onto the plate, allowing the pineapple slices and brown sugar topping to become the top of the cake.
12. Let the cake cool slightly before slicing and serving.
13. Serve the pineapple upside-down cake warm or at room temperature, optionally with a scoop of vanilla ice cream or a dollop of whipped cream.

Enjoy this classic pineapple upside-down cake with its sweet, caramelized topping and tender cake crumb—a perfect dessert for any occasion!

Black Forest Cake

Ingredients:

For the chocolate sponge cake:

- 1 3/4 cups all-purpose flour
- 3/4 cup unsweetened cocoa powder
- 1 3/4 cups granulated sugar
- 2 teaspoons baking powder
- 1 teaspoon baking soda
- 1 teaspoon salt
- 2 large eggs
- 1 cup buttermilk
- 1/2 cup vegetable oil
- 2 teaspoons vanilla extract
- 1 cup hot water

For the cherry filling:

- 2 cups pitted cherries (fresh or canned)
- 1/4 cup granulated sugar
- 1 tablespoon cornstarch
- 1 tablespoon water
- 1 tablespoon lemon juice

For the whipped cream:

- 2 cups heavy cream, chilled
- 1/4 cup powdered sugar
- 1 teaspoon vanilla extract

For decoration:

- Dark chocolate shavings
- Maraschino cherries

Instructions:

1. Preheat your oven to 350°F (175°C). Grease and flour two 9-inch round cake pans or line them with parchment paper.
2. In a large mixing bowl, sift together the flour, cocoa powder, granulated sugar, baking powder, baking soda, and salt.
3. In a separate mixing bowl, whisk together the eggs, buttermilk, vegetable oil, and vanilla extract until well combined.
4. Gradually add the wet ingredients to the dry ingredients, mixing until just combined. Then, gradually stir in the hot water until the batter is smooth.
5. Divide the batter evenly between the prepared cake pans and smooth the tops with a spatula.
6. Bake in the preheated oven for 25 to 30 minutes, or until a toothpick inserted into the center of the cakes comes out clean.
7. Remove the cakes from the oven and let them cool in the pans for 10 minutes before transferring them to wire racks to cool completely.
8. While the cakes are cooling, prepare the cherry filling. In a saucepan, combine the pitted cherries, granulated sugar, and lemon juice. Cook over medium heat until the cherries release their juices and soften, about 5-7 minutes.
9. In a small bowl, mix together the cornstarch and water to make a slurry. Stir the slurry into the cherry mixture and cook for an additional 2-3 minutes, until the filling thickens. Remove from heat and let it cool completely.
10. In a mixing bowl, beat the chilled heavy cream, powdered sugar, and vanilla extract until stiff peaks form.
11. Once the cakes and cherry filling have cooled, assemble the Black Forest cake. Place one layer of chocolate sponge cake on a serving plate or cake stand. Spread a layer of whipped cream over the cake layer, then spoon some of the cherry filling over the whipped cream.
12. Place the second layer of chocolate sponge cake on top and press down gently. Spread a layer of whipped cream over the top of the cake, then use the remaining cherry filling to decorate the top.
13. Garnish the cake with dark chocolate shavings and maraschino cherries.
14. Chill the assembled cake in the refrigerator for at least 1 hour before serving to allow the flavors to meld together.
15. Serve and enjoy this indulgent Black Forest cake as a decadent dessert!

This classic Black Forest cake is sure to impress with its layers of moist chocolate cake, creamy whipped cream, and sweet cherry filling—a perfect treat for any special occasion.

Pecan Pie

Ingredients:

For the pie crust:

- 1 1/4 cups all-purpose flour
- 1/2 teaspoon salt
- 1/2 teaspoon granulated sugar
- 1/2 cup unsalted butter, cold and cubed
- 3 to 4 tablespoons ice water

For the filling:

- 1 cup granulated sugar
- 1 cup light corn syrup
- 1/4 cup unsalted butter, melted
- 3 large eggs
- 1 teaspoon vanilla extract
- 1/4 teaspoon salt
- 1 1/2 cups pecan halves

Instructions:

1. Start by making the pie crust. In a large mixing bowl, whisk together the flour, salt, and granulated sugar.
2. Add the cold, cubed butter to the flour mixture. Use a pastry cutter or your fingers to cut the butter into the flour until the mixture resembles coarse crumbs.
3. Gradually add the ice water, one tablespoon at a time, mixing with a fork until the dough comes together and forms a ball. Be careful not to overwork the dough.
4. Shape the dough into a disk, wrap it in plastic wrap, and refrigerate for at least 30 minutes.
5. Preheat your oven to 375°F (190°C).
6. Roll out the chilled pie crust on a lightly floured surface into a circle about 12 inches in diameter. Carefully transfer the dough to a 9-inch pie dish, pressing it

gently into the bottom and up the sides. Trim any excess dough and crimp the edges as desired.
7. In a medium mixing bowl, whisk together the granulated sugar, corn syrup, melted butter, eggs, vanilla extract, and salt until well combined.
8. Arrange the pecan halves evenly over the bottom of the prepared pie crust.
9. Pour the filling mixture over the pecans, making sure they are evenly coated.
10. Place the pie in the preheated oven and bake for 45 to 50 minutes, or until the filling is set and the crust is golden brown. If the edges of the crust start to brown too quickly, you can cover them with aluminum foil halfway through baking.
11. Remove the pie from the oven and let it cool completely on a wire rack before slicing and serving.
12. Serve slices of pecan pie on their own or with a dollop of whipped cream or a scoop of vanilla ice cream, if desired.

Enjoy this classic pecan pie with its buttery crust and sweet, nutty filling—a perfect dessert for Thanksgiving or any special occasion!

Chocolate Truffles

Ingredients:

- 8 ounces (about 225g) semi-sweet or bittersweet chocolate, chopped
- 1/2 cup (120ml) heavy cream
- 1 tablespoon unsalted butter, softened
- 1 teaspoon vanilla extract
- Cocoa powder, powdered sugar, chopped nuts, or shredded coconut for coating (optional)

Instructions:

1. Place the chopped chocolate in a heatproof bowl. Set aside.
2. In a small saucepan, heat the heavy cream over medium heat until it just begins to simmer. Do not let it boil.
3. Pour the hot cream over the chopped chocolate. Let it sit undisturbed for 1-2 minutes to soften the chocolate.
4. Gently stir the chocolate and cream together until smooth and well combined. If needed, you can place the bowl over a pot of simmering water (double boiler) to help melt any remaining chocolate.
5. Stir in the softened butter and vanilla extract until fully incorporated.
6. Cover the bowl with plastic wrap and refrigerate the chocolate ganache for at least 2 hours, or until firm enough to scoop.
7. Once the ganache is chilled and firm, use a small spoon or a melon baller to scoop out small portions of ganache.
8. Roll each portion of ganache between your palms to form smooth balls. Place the rolled truffles on a baking sheet lined with parchment paper.
9. If desired, roll the truffles in cocoa powder, powdered sugar, chopped nuts, or shredded coconut to coat them. You can also leave some truffles plain or dip them in melted chocolate for an extra layer of richness.
10. Once all the truffles are coated, return them to the refrigerator for about 15-20 minutes to set.
11. Store the chocolate truffles in an airtight container in the refrigerator for up to two weeks. Bring them to room temperature before serving for the best texture and flavor.

12. Enjoy these homemade chocolate truffles as a decadent treat or gift them to friends and family for a special occasion!

Feel free to experiment with different types of chocolate, coatings, and flavorings to customize your chocolate truffles to your liking. They're perfect for indulging yourself or sharing with loved ones.

Tiramisu

Ingredients:

- 1 cup brewed strong coffee, cooled to room temperature
- 2 tablespoons coffee liqueur (optional)
- 3 large eggs, separated
- 3/4 cup granulated sugar, divided
- 1 teaspoon vanilla extract
- 8 ounces (about 1 cup) mascarpone cheese, softened
- 1 cup heavy cream
- 24-30 ladyfinger cookies (savoiardi)
- Unsweetened cocoa powder, for dusting

Instructions:

1. In a shallow dish, combine the brewed coffee and coffee liqueur (if using). Set aside.
2. In a mixing bowl, beat the egg yolks with 1/2 cup of granulated sugar until pale and creamy. Stir in the vanilla extract.
3. Add the softened mascarpone cheese to the egg yolk mixture and beat until smooth and well combined.
4. In a separate mixing bowl, beat the egg whites until soft peaks form. Gradually add the remaining 1/4 cup of granulated sugar and continue beating until stiff peaks form.
5. In another mixing bowl, whip the heavy cream until stiff peaks form.
6. Gently fold the whipped cream into the mascarpone mixture until smooth and well combined.
7. Gently fold the beaten egg whites into the mascarpone mixture until no streaks remain.
8. Dip each ladyfinger into the coffee mixture for a few seconds, ensuring they are evenly soaked but not overly saturated.
9. Arrange a layer of soaked ladyfingers in the bottom of a 9x13-inch dish or a trifle dish, breaking them as needed to fit.
10. Spread half of the mascarpone mixture over the layer of soaked ladyfingers, smoothing it out with a spatula.

11. Repeat the process with another layer of soaked ladyfingers followed by the remaining mascarpone mixture.
12. Cover the dish with plastic wrap and refrigerate the tiramisu for at least 4 hours, or overnight, to allow the flavors to meld and the dessert to set.
13. Before serving, dust the top of the tiramisu with unsweetened cocoa powder using a fine-mesh sieve.
14. Slice and serve the tiramisu chilled, and enjoy this classic Italian dessert with its rich, creamy texture and coffee-infused flavor!

Tiramisu is a perfect dessert for special occasions or dinner parties, and it's sure to impress with its elegant presentation and delicious taste.

Funfetti Sugar Cookies

Ingredients:

- 1 cup unsalted butter, softened
- 1 cup granulated sugar
- 2 large eggs
- 2 teaspoons vanilla extract
- 3 cups all-purpose flour
- 1 teaspoon baking powder
- 1/2 teaspoon salt
- 1/2 cup rainbow sprinkles (plus extra for topping, if desired)

Instructions:

1. Preheat your oven to 350°F (175°C). Line baking sheets with parchment paper or silicone baking mats.
2. In a large mixing bowl, cream together the softened butter and granulated sugar until light and fluffy.
3. Beat in the eggs, one at a time, until well combined. Stir in the vanilla extract.
4. In a separate bowl, whisk together the flour, baking powder, and salt.
5. Gradually add the dry ingredients to the wet ingredients, mixing until just combined.
6. Gently fold in the rainbow sprinkles until evenly distributed throughout the dough. Be careful not to overmix, as this can cause the colors to bleed.
7. Using a cookie scoop or spoon, portion the dough into balls and place them onto the prepared baking sheets, spacing them about 2 inches apart.
8. Flatten each dough ball slightly with the palm of your hand or the bottom of a glass.
9. If desired, press a few extra sprinkles onto the tops of the cookies for a fun and colorful appearance.
10. Bake in the preheated oven for 10-12 minutes, or until the edges are set and the cookies are just beginning to turn golden brown.
11. Remove the cookies from the oven and let them cool on the baking sheets for a few minutes before transferring them to wire racks to cool completely.
12. Once cooled, serve and enjoy these delightful funfetti sugar cookies as a sweet treat or snack!

These funfetti sugar cookies are perfect for birthday parties, celebrations, or any occasion where you want to add a touch of color and fun to your dessert spread. They're sure to be a hit with kids and adults alike!

Salted Caramel Brownies

Ingredients:

For the brownie layer:

- 1 cup (2 sticks) unsalted butter
- 2 cups granulated sugar
- 4 large eggs
- 1 teaspoon vanilla extract
- 1 cup all-purpose flour
- 3/4 cup unsweetened cocoa powder
- 1/2 teaspoon salt

For the salted caramel layer:

- 1 cup granulated sugar
- 6 tablespoons unsalted butter, cut into pieces
- 1/2 cup heavy cream
- 1 teaspoon vanilla extract
- 1 teaspoon sea salt, plus extra for sprinkling

Instructions:

1. Preheat your oven to 350°F (175°C). Grease a 9x13-inch baking pan or line it with parchment paper, leaving some overhang on the sides for easy removal.
2. In a medium saucepan, melt the butter over low heat. Remove from heat and stir in the granulated sugar until well combined.
3. Whisk in the eggs, one at a time, until incorporated. Stir in the vanilla extract.
4. In a separate bowl, sift together the flour, cocoa powder, and salt. Gradually add the dry ingredients to the wet ingredients, mixing until just combined.
5. Pour the brownie batter into the prepared baking pan and spread it out evenly with a spatula.
6. To make the salted caramel layer, place the granulated sugar in a medium saucepan over medium heat. Stir occasionally with a heatproof spatula until the sugar melts and turns amber in color.

7. Once the sugar has melted and caramelized, add the butter to the saucepan and stir until melted and well combined.
8. Carefully pour in the heavy cream while stirring constantly. Be careful, as the mixture will bubble up.
9. Continue to cook the caramel mixture for another 2-3 minutes, stirring constantly, until smooth and slightly thickened.
10. Remove the saucepan from heat and stir in the vanilla extract and sea salt.
11. Pour the salted caramel sauce over the brownie batter in the baking pan, spreading it out evenly with a spatula.
12. Use a knife or skewer to gently swirl the salted caramel into the brownie batter.
13. Bake in the preheated oven for 25-30 minutes, or until the edges are set and a toothpick inserted into the center comes out with a few moist crumbs.
14. Remove the brownies from the oven and sprinkle with additional sea salt, if desired.
15. Let the brownies cool completely in the pan on a wire rack before slicing and serving.
16. Enjoy these indulgent salted caramel brownies as a decadent dessert or snack!

These salted caramel brownies are sure to satisfy your sweet and salty cravings with their rich chocolatey flavor and gooey caramel goodness. They're perfect for special occasions or whenever you're in need of a sweet treat!

Peanut Butter Cupcakes

Ingredients:

For the cupcakes:

- 1 1/2 cups all-purpose flour
- 1 1/2 teaspoons baking powder
- 1/4 teaspoon salt
- 1/2 cup unsalted butter, softened
- 1 cup granulated sugar
- 2 large eggs
- 1 teaspoon vanilla extract
- 1/2 cup creamy peanut butter
- 1/2 cup whole milk

For the peanut butter frosting:

- 1/2 cup unsalted butter, softened
- 1 cup creamy peanut butter
- 2 cups powdered sugar
- 2-3 tablespoons whole milk
- 1 teaspoon vanilla extract

Instructions:

1. Preheat your oven to 350°F (175°C). Line a muffin tin with cupcake liners.
2. In a medium mixing bowl, whisk together the flour, baking powder, and salt. Set aside.
3. In a large mixing bowl, cream together the softened butter and granulated sugar until light and fluffy.
4. Beat in the eggs, one at a time, until well combined. Stir in the vanilla extract.
5. Add the creamy peanut butter to the butter-sugar mixture and beat until smooth and creamy.

6. Gradually add the dry ingredients to the wet ingredients, alternating with the milk, beginning and ending with the dry ingredients. Mix until just combined, being careful not to overmix.
7. Divide the cupcake batter evenly among the prepared muffin cups, filling each about two-thirds full.
8. Bake in the preheated oven for 18-20 minutes, or until a toothpick inserted into the center of a cupcake comes out clean.
9. Remove the cupcakes from the oven and let them cool in the muffin tin for a few minutes before transferring them to a wire rack to cool completely.
10. While the cupcakes are cooling, prepare the peanut butter frosting. In a large mixing bowl, beat together the softened butter and creamy peanut butter until smooth and creamy.
11. Gradually add the powdered sugar, mixing until well combined and smooth.
12. Add the whole milk, one tablespoon at a time, until the frosting reaches your desired consistency. Stir in the vanilla extract.
13. Once the cupcakes are completely cooled, pipe or spread the peanut butter frosting onto the cupcakes.
14. Optional: garnish each cupcake with chopped peanuts, mini chocolate chips, or a drizzle of melted chocolate.
15. Serve and enjoy these delicious peanut butter cupcakes as a delightful dessert or snack!

These peanut butter cupcakes are sure to please any peanut butter lover with their rich, nutty flavor and creamy frosting. They're perfect for birthday parties, bake sales, or any occasion where you want to indulge in a sweet treat!

Mocha Chocolate Chip Cookies

Ingredients:

- 1 cup (2 sticks) unsalted butter, softened
- 3/4 cup granulated sugar
- 3/4 cup packed brown sugar
- 2 large eggs
- 1 teaspoon vanilla extract
- 2 cups all-purpose flour
- 1/2 cup unsweetened cocoa powder
- 1 tablespoon instant espresso powder or instant coffee granules
- 1 teaspoon baking soda
- 1/2 teaspoon salt
- 1 1/2 cups semisweet chocolate chips

Instructions:

1. Preheat your oven to 350°F (175°C). Line baking sheets with parchment paper or silicone baking mats.
2. In a small bowl, dissolve the instant espresso powder or coffee granules in 1 tablespoon of hot water. Set aside to cool slightly.
3. In a large mixing bowl, cream together the softened butter, granulated sugar, and brown sugar until light and fluffy.
4. Beat in the eggs, one at a time, until well combined. Stir in the vanilla extract and the dissolved espresso or coffee mixture.
5. In a separate bowl, whisk together the flour, cocoa powder, baking soda, and salt.
6. Gradually add the dry ingredients to the wet ingredients, mixing until just combined.
7. Stir in the semisweet chocolate chips until evenly distributed throughout the cookie dough.
8. Using a cookie scoop or spoon, drop tablespoon-sized portions of dough onto the prepared baking sheets, spacing them about 2 inches apart.
9. Flatten each dough ball slightly with the palm of your hand or the bottom of a glass.
10. Bake in the preheated oven for 8-10 minutes, or until the edges are set and the cookies are slightly firm to the touch.

11. Remove the cookies from the oven and let them cool on the baking sheets for a few minutes before transferring them to wire racks to cool completely.
12. Once cooled, serve and enjoy these delicious mocha chocolate chip cookies with a glass of milk or a cup of coffee!

These mocha chocolate chip cookies are perfect for coffee lovers and chocolate enthusiasts alike, with their rich, indulgent flavor and soft, chewy texture. They're great for sharing with friends and family or enjoying as a special treat for yourself!

Cherry Pie

Ingredients:

For the pie crust:

- 2 1/2 cups all-purpose flour
- 1 teaspoon salt
- 1 tablespoon granulated sugar
- 1 cup (2 sticks) unsalted butter, cold and cut into cubes
- 6-8 tablespoons ice water

For the cherry filling:

- 5 cups fresh or frozen cherries, pitted
- 3/4 cup granulated sugar
- 1/4 cup cornstarch
- 1 tablespoon lemon juice
- 1/2 teaspoon almond extract (optional)
- 1/4 teaspoon salt
- 1 tablespoon unsalted butter, cut into small pieces

Instructions:

1. Start by making the pie crust. In a large mixing bowl, whisk together the flour, salt, and granulated sugar.
2. Add the cold, cubed butter to the flour mixture. Use a pastry cutter or your fingers to cut the butter into the flour until the mixture resembles coarse crumbs with some pea-sized pieces of butter remaining.
3. Gradually add the ice water, one tablespoon at a time, mixing with a fork until the dough just begins to come together. Be careful not to overwork the dough.
4. Divide the dough in half and shape each half into a disk. Wrap each disk tightly in plastic wrap and refrigerate for at least 1 hour, or until chilled.
5. While the dough is chilling, preheat your oven to 400°F (200°C). Place a baking sheet in the oven to preheat as well.

6. In a large mixing bowl, combine the pitted cherries, granulated sugar, cornstarch, lemon juice, almond extract (if using), and salt. Stir until the cherries are evenly coated.
7. Roll out one disk of chilled pie dough on a lightly floured surface into a circle about 12 inches in diameter. Carefully transfer the dough to a 9-inch pie dish, pressing it gently into the bottom and up the sides.
8. Pour the cherry filling into the prepared pie crust, spreading it out evenly.
9. Dot the top of the cherry filling with small pieces of unsalted butter.
10. Roll out the second disk of chilled pie dough into a circle about 12 inches in diameter. Carefully place it over the cherry filling.
11. Trim any excess dough from the edges and crimp the edges as desired to seal the pie.
12. Cut several slits in the top crust to allow steam to escape during baking.
13. Place the pie on the preheated baking sheet in the oven and bake for 45-55 minutes, or until the crust is golden brown and the filling is bubbling.
14. If the edges of the crust start to brown too quickly, you can cover them with aluminum foil halfway through baking.
15. Once baked, remove the pie from the oven and let it cool on a wire rack for at least 2 hours before slicing and serving.
16. Serve slices of cherry pie on their own or with a scoop of vanilla ice cream for a delicious dessert!

Enjoy this classic cherry pie with its sweet and tangy filling and flaky pastry crust—a perfect treat for any occasion, especially during cherry season!

Almond Joy Bars

Ingredients:

For the coconut filling:

- 2 1/2 cups shredded coconut (sweetened or unsweetened)
- 1/2 cup sweetened condensed milk
- 1/2 cup powdered sugar
- 1/2 teaspoon vanilla extract
- 1/4 teaspoon almond extract
- 1/2 cup whole almonds, toasted

For the chocolate coating:

- 10 ounces (about 1 2/3 cups) semisweet chocolate chips
- 2 tablespoons coconut oil

Instructions:

1. Line an 8x8-inch baking dish with parchment paper, leaving some overhang on the sides for easy removal of the bars later.
2. In a large mixing bowl, combine the shredded coconut, sweetened condensed milk, powdered sugar, vanilla extract, and almond extract. Stir until well combined and the mixture holds together when pressed.
3. Press half of the coconut mixture evenly into the bottom of the prepared baking dish.
4. Place the whole almonds evenly over the coconut layer, pressing them gently into the mixture.
5. Spread the remaining coconut mixture over the almonds, pressing it down firmly to create a smooth, even layer.
6. In a microwave-safe bowl, combine the semisweet chocolate chips and coconut oil. Microwave in 30-second intervals, stirring between each interval, until the chocolate is melted and smooth.
7. Pour the melted chocolate over the coconut layer, spreading it out evenly with a spatula.
8. Place the baking dish in the refrigerator for about 1 hour, or until the chocolate is set.

9. Once the chocolate is set, use the parchment paper to lift the bars out of the baking dish. Place them on a cutting board and cut into bars or squares using a sharp knife.
10. Store the Almond Joy bars in an airtight container in the refrigerator for up to one week.
11. Serve and enjoy these homemade Almond Joy bars as a delicious treat!

These homemade Almond Joy bars are sure to satisfy your craving for the classic candy bar with their sweet coconut filling, crunchy almonds, and rich chocolate coating. They're perfect for snacking, sharing, or gifting to friends and family!

Lemon Meringue Pie

Ingredients:

For the pie crust:

- 1 1/4 cups all-purpose flour
- 1/2 teaspoon salt
- 1/2 cup (1 stick) unsalted butter, chilled and cut into small pieces
- 3 to 4 tablespoons ice water

For the lemon filling:

- 1 cup granulated sugar
- 1/4 cup cornstarch
- 1/4 teaspoon salt
- 1 1/2 cups water
- 4 large egg yolks
- 1 tablespoon lemon zest
- 1/2 cup freshly squeezed lemon juice (about 3-4 lemons)
- 2 tablespoons unsalted butter

For the meringue topping:

- 4 large egg whites, at room temperature
- 1/4 teaspoon cream of tartar
- 1/2 cup granulated sugar

Instructions:

1. Start by making the pie crust. In a food processor, combine the flour and salt. Add the chilled butter pieces and pulse until the mixture resembles coarse crumbs.
2. Gradually add the ice water, 1 tablespoon at a time, pulsing until the dough just begins to come together.
3. Turn the dough out onto a lightly floured surface and gather it into a ball. Flatten the dough into a disk, wrap it in plastic wrap, and refrigerate for at least 1 hour.

4. Preheat your oven to 375°F (190°C). Roll out the chilled pie dough on a lightly floured surface into a circle about 12 inches in diameter. Carefully transfer the dough to a 9-inch pie dish, pressing it gently into the bottom and up the sides. Trim any excess dough and crimp the edges as desired.
5. Prick the bottom of the pie crust with a fork and line it with parchment paper. Fill the pie crust with pie weights or dried beans.
6. Bake the pie crust in the preheated oven for 15 minutes. Remove the pie weights and parchment paper, then bake for an additional 5-7 minutes, or until the crust is lightly golden brown. Remove from the oven and let cool while you prepare the filling.
7. To make the lemon filling, in a medium saucepan, whisk together the granulated sugar, cornstarch, and salt. Gradually whisk in the water until smooth.
8. Place the saucepan over medium heat and cook, stirring constantly, until the mixture thickens and comes to a boil. Boil for 1 minute, then remove from heat.
9. In a separate bowl, whisk the egg yolks until smooth. Gradually whisk in about 1/2 cup of the hot sugar mixture to temper the eggs, then pour the egg mixture back into the saucepan, whisking constantly.
10. Return the saucepan to medium heat and cook, stirring constantly, until the mixture thickens again, about 2-3 minutes.
11. Remove the saucepan from heat and stir in the lemon zest, lemon juice, and unsalted butter until the butter is melted and the mixture is smooth.
12. Pour the lemon filling into the baked pie crust and smooth the top with a spatula. Set aside while you prepare the meringue topping.
13. To make the meringue topping, in a clean mixing bowl, beat the egg whites and cream of tartar on medium speed until soft peaks form.
14. Gradually add the granulated sugar, a tablespoon at a time, while continuing to beat on high speed, until stiff, glossy peaks form.
15. Spread the meringue over the warm lemon filling, making sure to spread it all the way to the edges of the pie crust to seal in the filling.
16. Use the back of a spoon to create peaks in the meringue.
17. Bake the pie in the preheated oven for 10-12 minutes, or until the meringue is lightly golden brown.
18. Remove the pie from the oven and let it cool completely on a wire rack before serving.
19. Once cooled, slice and serve this delicious lemon meringue pie as a delightful dessert!

This homemade lemon meringue pie is sure to impress with its tangy lemon filling and fluffy meringue topping—a perfect dessert for any occasion!

Chocolate Covered Strawberries

Ingredients:

- Fresh strawberries, washed and dried (choose ones with intact stems for easy dipping)
- High-quality chocolate (dark, milk, or white), chopped or in chips
- Optional: Additional toppings such as chopped nuts, shredded coconut, sprinkles, or edible glitter

Instructions:

1. Line a baking sheet or large plate with parchment paper or wax paper. This will be used to place the chocolate-covered strawberries on to set.
2. Prepare your toppings, if using, by placing them in small bowls or plates. You'll want to have them ready before you start dipping the strawberries.
3. In a heatproof bowl, melt the chocolate using one of the following methods:
    - Microwave: Place the chocolate in a microwave-safe bowl and heat in 30-second intervals, stirring between each interval, until melted and smooth.
    - Double boiler: Place the chocolate in a heatproof bowl set over a pot of simmering water. Stir the chocolate occasionally until melted and smooth.
4. Hold a strawberry by the stem and dip it into the melted chocolate, swirling to coat it completely. Allow any excess chocolate to drip back into the bowl.
5. If desired, immediately roll the chocolate-covered strawberry in your chosen toppings while the chocolate is still wet.
6. Place the dipped strawberries onto the prepared baking sheet or plate, making sure they are not touching each other.
7. Repeat the dipping process with the remaining strawberries until they are all coated in chocolate.
8. Once all the strawberries are dipped, place the baking sheet or plate in the refrigerator for about 15-30 minutes, or until the chocolate has set.
9. Once the chocolate has set, remove the chocolate-covered strawberries from the refrigerator and transfer them to a serving plate or platter.
10. Serve the chocolate-covered strawberries immediately, or store them in the refrigerator for up to 24 hours before serving. Enjoy!

These homemade chocolate-covered strawberries are sure to impress with their glossy chocolate coating and fresh, juicy strawberries. They make a beautiful and delicious addition to any dessert table or romantic gesture.

Mint Chocolate Chip Ice Cream

Ingredients:

- 2 cups heavy cream
- 1 cup whole milk
- 3/4 cup granulated sugar
- 1 teaspoon pure vanilla extract
- 1 teaspoon peppermint extract
- Green food coloring (optional)
- 1 cup semisweet chocolate chips or chopped chocolate
- Fresh mint leaves for garnish (optional)

Instructions:

1. In a large mixing bowl, whisk together the heavy cream, whole milk, granulated sugar, vanilla extract, and peppermint extract until the sugar is dissolved and the mixture is well combined.
2. If desired, add a few drops of green food coloring to achieve the desired mint color. Stir until evenly distributed.
3. Cover the bowl with plastic wrap and refrigerate the mixture for at least 1 hour, or until thoroughly chilled.
4. Once chilled, pour the mixture into the bowl of an ice cream maker and churn according to the manufacturer's instructions until it reaches a soft-serve consistency.
5. In the last few minutes of churning, add the semisweet chocolate chips or chopped chocolate and continue churning until evenly distributed.
6. Transfer the churned ice cream to a freezer-safe container, layering it with additional chocolate chips if desired. Use a spatula to smooth the top.
7. Cover the container with a lid or plastic wrap and freeze the ice cream for at least 4 hours, or until firm.
8. Once the ice cream is fully frozen, scoop it into bowls or cones and garnish with fresh mint leaves if desired.
9. Serve and enjoy this refreshing mint chocolate chip ice cream as a delightful dessert!

This homemade mint chocolate chip ice cream is sure to impress with its creamy texture and refreshing mint flavor, studded with bursts of rich chocolate throughout. It's perfect for enjoying on its own, as a topping for brownies or pie, or in an ice cream sandwich.

Peach Cobbler

Ingredients:

For the peach filling:

- 6 cups fresh or frozen peaches, peeled and sliced (about 6-8 peaches)
- 1 cup granulated sugar
- 1/4 cup brown sugar
- 1/4 teaspoon ground cinnamon
- 1/8 teaspoon ground nutmeg
- 1 tablespoon lemon juice
- 2 tablespoons cornstarch

For the biscuit topping:

- 1 1/2 cups all-purpose flour
- 1/2 cup granulated sugar
- 2 teaspoons baking powder
- 1/2 teaspoon salt
- 1/2 cup (1 stick) unsalted butter, cold and cut into small pieces
- 1/2 cup milk
- 1 teaspoon vanilla extract

Instructions:

1. Preheat your oven to 375°F (190°C). Grease a 9x13-inch baking dish or a similar-sized baking dish with butter or cooking spray.
2. In a large mixing bowl, combine the sliced peaches, granulated sugar, brown sugar, ground cinnamon, ground nutmeg, lemon juice, and cornstarch. Stir until the peaches are evenly coated in the sugar mixture.
3. Pour the peach filling into the prepared baking dish, spreading it out evenly.
4. In a separate mixing bowl, whisk together the all-purpose flour, granulated sugar, baking powder, and salt.
5. Cut the cold butter into the flour mixture using a pastry cutter or your fingers, until the mixture resembles coarse crumbs.

6. In a small bowl, combine the milk and vanilla extract. Gradually add the milk mixture to the flour mixture, stirring until a soft dough forms.
7. Drop spoonfuls of the biscuit dough evenly over the top of the peach filling in the baking dish.
8. Bake in the preheated oven for 40-45 minutes, or until the peach filling is bubbly and the biscuit topping is golden brown and cooked through.
9. Remove the peach cobbler from the oven and let it cool for a few minutes before serving.
10. Serve the peach cobbler warm, either on its own or with a scoop of vanilla ice cream or a dollop of whipped cream.
11. Enjoy this classic peach cobbler as a comforting and delicious dessert!

This homemade peach cobbler is sure to be a hit with its juicy peach filling and buttery biscuit topping. It's a perfect dessert for summer gatherings, potlucks, or any occasion where you want to impress with a homemade treat.

Nutella Swirl Pound Cake

Ingredients:

- 1 cup (2 sticks) unsalted butter, softened
- 1 1/2 cups granulated sugar
- 4 large eggs
- 2 teaspoons vanilla extract
- 2 cups all-purpose flour
- 1/2 teaspoon baking powder
- 1/4 teaspoon salt
- 1/2 cup milk
- 1/2 cup Nutella

Instructions:

1. Preheat your oven to 350°F (175°C). Grease and flour a 9x5-inch loaf pan or line it with parchment paper for easy removal.
2. In a large mixing bowl, cream together the softened butter and granulated sugar until light and fluffy.
3. Beat in the eggs, one at a time, until well combined. Stir in the vanilla extract.
4. In a separate bowl, whisk together the flour, baking powder, and salt.
5. Gradually add the dry ingredients to the wet ingredients, alternating with the milk, beginning and ending with the dry ingredients. Mix until just combined, being careful not to overmix.
6. Pour half of the batter into the prepared loaf pan, spreading it out evenly with a spatula.
7. Warm the Nutella in the microwave for a few seconds to soften it, then spoon half of it over the batter in the loaf pan.
8. Use a knife or skewer to gently swirl the Nutella into the batter, creating a marbled effect.
9. Repeat the process with the remaining batter and Nutella, creating another layer of batter followed by Nutella swirls.
10. Use a knife or skewer to swirl the Nutella into the top layer of batter.
11. Bake in the preheated oven for 50-60 minutes, or until a toothpick inserted into the center comes out clean.

12. If the top of the cake starts to brown too quickly, you can tent it loosely with aluminum foil halfway through baking.
13. Once baked, remove the pound cake from the oven and let it cool in the pan for 10-15 minutes before transferring it to a wire rack to cool completely.
14. Once cooled, slice and serve this delicious Nutella swirl pound cake as a delightful dessert or snack!

This Nutella swirl pound cake is sure to please with its rich, chocolatey Nutella swirls and tender, buttery crumb. It's perfect for enjoying with a cup of coffee or tea, or as a sweet treat for any occasion!

White Chocolate Raspberry Cheesecake

Ingredients:

For the crust:

- 1 1/2 cups graham cracker crumbs (about 12-14 graham crackers)
- 1/4 cup granulated sugar
- 1/2 cup unsalted butter, melted

For the raspberry sauce:

- 1 1/2 cups fresh or frozen raspberries
- 1/4 cup granulated sugar
- 1 tablespoon lemon juice
- 1 tablespoon cornstarch

For the cheesecake filling:

- 24 ounces (3 packages) cream cheese, softened
- 1 cup granulated sugar
- 3 large eggs
- 1 teaspoon vanilla extract
- 8 ounces white chocolate, melted and cooled slightly
- 1/2 cup sour cream

For garnish (optional):

- Fresh raspberries
- White chocolate curls or shavings

Instructions:

1. Preheat your oven to 325°F (160°C). Grease a 9-inch springform pan and wrap the bottom in aluminum foil to prevent any leaks.
2. In a mixing bowl, combine the graham cracker crumbs, granulated sugar, and melted butter. Stir until the crumbs are evenly moistened.

3. Press the crumb mixture firmly into the bottom of the prepared springform pan, using the back of a spoon or the bottom of a glass to create an even layer. Set aside.
4. To make the raspberry sauce, combine the raspberries, granulated sugar, lemon juice, and cornstarch in a saucepan set over medium heat. Cook, stirring occasionally, until the raspberries break down and the sauce thickens, about 5-7 minutes. Remove from heat and let cool slightly.
5. Strain the raspberry sauce through a fine-mesh sieve to remove the seeds, pressing down with the back of a spoon to extract as much sauce as possible. Set aside to cool completely.
6. In a large mixing bowl, beat the softened cream cheese and granulated sugar together until smooth and creamy.
7. Add the eggs one at a time, beating well after each addition. Stir in the vanilla extract.
8. Gradually pour in the melted white chocolate, mixing until smooth and well combined.
9. Fold in the sour cream until evenly incorporated into the cheesecake batter.
10. Pour half of the cheesecake batter over the prepared crust in the springform pan, spreading it out evenly with a spatula.
11. Drizzle half of the raspberry sauce over the cheesecake batter in the pan, using a spoon or spatula to swirl it into the batter.
12. Repeat with the remaining cheesecake batter and raspberry sauce, creating another layer of batter followed by swirls of raspberry sauce.
13. Place the springform pan in a larger baking dish or roasting pan and add hot water to the larger dish until it comes about halfway up the sides of the springform pan. This water bath will help prevent the cheesecake from cracking during baking.
14. Bake the cheesecake in the preheated oven for 60-70 minutes, or until the edges are set and the center is slightly wobbly.
15. Turn off the oven and leave the cheesecake inside with the door slightly ajar for 1 hour to cool gradually.
16. Remove the cheesecake from the oven and transfer it to a wire rack to cool completely. Once cooled, refrigerate the cheesecake for at least 4 hours or overnight to set.
17. Before serving, garnish the chilled cheesecake with fresh raspberries and white chocolate curls or shavings if desired.
18. Slice and serve this delicious white chocolate raspberry cheesecake as a decadent dessert for any special occasion or celebration!

This white chocolate raspberry cheesecake is sure to impress with its creamy texture, vibrant raspberry swirls, and irresistible white chocolate flavor. It's perfect for sharing with friends and family or as a stunning centerpiece for your dessert table. Enjoy!

Apple Crisp

Ingredients:

For the apple filling:

- 6 cups peeled, cored, and sliced apples (such as Granny Smith or Honeycrisp)
- 1/4 cup granulated sugar
- 2 tablespoons all-purpose flour
- 1 teaspoon ground cinnamon
- 1/4 teaspoon ground nutmeg
- 1 tablespoon lemon juice

For the crisp topping:

- 1 cup old-fashioned rolled oats
- 1/2 cup all-purpose flour
- 1/2 cup packed brown sugar
- 1/4 teaspoon salt
- 1/2 cup (1 stick) unsalted butter, cold and cut into small pieces

Instructions:

1. Preheat your oven to 375°F (190°C). Grease a 9x9-inch baking dish or a similar-sized baking dish with butter or cooking spray.
2. In a large mixing bowl, combine the sliced apples, granulated sugar, all-purpose flour, ground cinnamon, ground nutmeg, and lemon juice. Toss until the apples are evenly coated in the sugar mixture.
3. Pour the apple mixture into the prepared baking dish, spreading it out evenly.
4. In a separate mixing bowl, combine the rolled oats, all-purpose flour, brown sugar, and salt. Stir until well combined.
5. Add the cold, cubed butter to the oat mixture. Use your fingers or a pastry cutter to work the butter into the dry ingredients until the mixture resembles coarse crumbs and the butter is evenly distributed.
6. Sprinkle the oat topping evenly over the apple mixture in the baking dish, covering it completely.

7. Bake in the preheated oven for 35-40 minutes, or until the topping is golden brown and the apples are tender and bubbly.
8. If the topping starts to brown too quickly, you can cover the baking dish loosely with aluminum foil halfway through baking.
9. Once baked, remove the apple crisp from the oven and let it cool for a few minutes before serving.
10. Serve the apple crisp warm, either on its own or with a scoop of vanilla ice cream or a dollop of whipped cream.
11. Enjoy this classic apple crisp as a comforting and delicious dessert!

This homemade apple crisp is sure to be a hit with its tender, spiced apples and crunchy oat topping. It's perfect for enjoying during the fall season or any time you're craving a warm and comforting dessert.

Caramel Popcorn

Ingredients:

- 10 cups popped popcorn (about 1/2 cup unpopped kernels)
- 1 cup unsalted butter
- 2 cups packed brown sugar
- 1/2 cup light corn syrup
- 1/2 teaspoon salt
- 1/2 teaspoon baking soda
- 1 teaspoon vanilla extract

Instructions:

1. Preheat your oven to 250°F (120°C). Line a large baking sheet with parchment paper or a silicone baking mat.
2. Place the popped popcorn in a large mixing bowl, removing any unpopped kernels. Set aside.
3. In a medium saucepan, melt the unsalted butter over medium heat.
4. Stir in the packed brown sugar, light corn syrup, and salt. Cook, stirring constantly, until the mixture comes to a boil.
5. Once the mixture is boiling, continue to cook without stirring for 4-5 minutes, or until it reaches a temperature of 235°F (113°C) on a candy thermometer. The mixture should be thick and bubbly.
6. Remove the saucepan from the heat and stir in the baking soda and vanilla extract. The mixture will foam up slightly.
7. Immediately pour the caramel mixture over the popped popcorn in the mixing bowl, stirring quickly to coat the popcorn evenly.
8. Spread the caramel-coated popcorn out in an even layer on the prepared baking sheet.
9. Bake the caramel popcorn in the preheated oven for 45-60 minutes, stirring every 15 minutes, until the popcorn is crisp and the caramel is set.
10. Remove the caramel popcorn from the oven and let it cool completely on the baking sheet.
11. Once cooled, break the caramel popcorn into clusters or pieces and store it in an airtight container at room temperature.
12. Serve and enjoy this delicious homemade caramel popcorn as a sweet and addictive snack!

This homemade caramel popcorn is sure to be a hit with its crunchy texture and rich caramel flavor. It's perfect for sharing with friends and family or enjoying on your own during a cozy movie night. Feel free to customize the recipe by adding nuts, chocolate chips, or other mix-ins for extra flavor and variety!

Pumpkin Pie

Ingredients:

For the pie crust:

- 1 1/4 cups all-purpose flour
- 1/2 teaspoon salt
- 1/2 cup (1 stick) unsalted butter, cold and cut into small cubes
- 1/4 cup ice water

For the pumpkin filling:

- 1 can (15 ounces) pumpkin puree (not pumpkin pie filling)
- 3/4 cup packed brown sugar
- 2 large eggs
- 1 cup evaporated milk (or half-and-half)
- 1 teaspoon vanilla extract
- 1 teaspoon ground cinnamon
- 1/2 teaspoon ground ginger
- 1/4 teaspoon ground nutmeg
- 1/4 teaspoon ground cloves
- 1/2 teaspoon salt

Instructions:

1. Preheat your oven to 375°F (190°C).
2. In a large mixing bowl, combine the all-purpose flour and salt for the pie crust. Add the cold, cubed butter.
3. Use a pastry cutter or your fingers to cut the butter into the flour until the mixture resembles coarse crumbs.
4. Gradually add the ice water, 1 tablespoon at a time, mixing with a fork, until the dough just comes together. Be careful not to overmix.
5. Shape the dough into a disk, wrap it in plastic wrap, and refrigerate for at least 30 minutes.

6. On a lightly floured surface, roll out the chilled dough into a circle about 12 inches in diameter. Carefully transfer the dough to a 9-inch pie dish, pressing it gently into the bottom and up the sides. Trim any excess dough and crimp the edges as desired.
7. In a large mixing bowl, whisk together the pumpkin puree, packed brown sugar, eggs, evaporated milk (or half-and-half), vanilla extract, ground cinnamon, ground ginger, ground nutmeg, ground cloves, and salt until smooth and well combined.
8. Pour the pumpkin filling into the prepared pie crust, spreading it out evenly.
9. Place the pie in the preheated oven and bake for 15 minutes.
10. After 15 minutes, reduce the oven temperature to 350°F (175°C) and continue baking for 40-50 minutes, or until the filling is set and a knife inserted into the center comes out clean.
11. If the edges of the crust start to brown too quickly, you can cover them with aluminum foil or a pie crust shield.
12. Once baked, remove the pie from the oven and let it cool completely on a wire rack before serving.
13. Serve slices of pumpkin pie on their own or with a dollop of whipped cream or a scoop of vanilla ice cream, if desired.
14. Enjoy this classic pumpkin pie as a delicious dessert, perfect for autumn gatherings and holiday celebrations!

This homemade pumpkin pie is sure to be a hit with its rich, spiced pumpkin filling and buttery pie crust. It's a comforting and festive dessert that's perfect for sharing with friends and family during the fall season.

Gingerbread Cookies

Ingredients:

- 3 cups all-purpose flour
- 1 teaspoon baking soda
- 1/4 teaspoon salt
- 1 tablespoon ground ginger
- 1 1/2 teaspoons ground cinnamon
- 1/4 teaspoon ground cloves
- 1/4 teaspoon ground nutmeg
- 3/4 cup unsalted butter, softened
- 1/2 cup packed brown sugar
- 1/2 cup granulated sugar
- 1/4 cup molasses
- 1 large egg
- 1 teaspoon vanilla extract

Instructions:

1. In a medium mixing bowl, whisk together the all-purpose flour, baking soda, salt, ground ginger, ground cinnamon, ground cloves, and ground nutmeg until well combined. Set aside.
2. In a large mixing bowl, cream together the softened unsalted butter, packed brown sugar, and granulated sugar until light and fluffy.
3. Add the molasses, egg, and vanilla extract to the butter mixture, and beat until well combined.
4. Gradually add the dry ingredients to the wet ingredients, mixing until a soft dough forms. If the dough is too sticky, you can add a little more flour, 1 tablespoon at a time, until it reaches the desired consistency.
5. Divide the dough into two equal portions, flatten each portion into a disk, wrap them in plastic wrap, and refrigerate for at least 1 hour or until firm.
6. Preheat your oven to 350°F (175°C). Line baking sheets with parchment paper or silicone baking mats.
7. On a lightly floured surface, roll out one portion of the chilled dough to about 1/4-inch thickness. Use gingerbread cookie cutters to cut out shapes, then transfer the cookies to the prepared baking sheets, spacing them about 1 inch apart.

8. Gather any scraps of dough, reroll them, and cut out more cookies until all the dough is used.
9. Bake the cookies in the preheated oven for 8-10 minutes, or until the edges are set and the cookies are lightly golden brown.
10. Remove the cookies from the oven and let them cool on the baking sheets for a few minutes before transferring them to a wire rack to cool completely.
11. Once cooled, decorate the gingerbread cookies with royal icing, if desired, or serve them plain.
12. Store the gingerbread cookies in an airtight container at room temperature for up to one week.

Enjoy these homemade gingerbread cookies as a festive and delicious treat during the holiday season! They're perfect for decorating with icing or enjoying on their own with a cup of hot cocoa.

Cranberry Orange Bread

Ingredients:

- 2 cups all-purpose flour
- 1 cup granulated sugar
- 1 1/2 teaspoons baking powder
- 1/2 teaspoon baking soda
- 1/2 teaspoon salt
- 1 cup fresh cranberries, chopped
- Zest of 1 orange
- 1/2 cup unsalted butter, melted and cooled
- 2 large eggs
- 3/4 cup orange juice
- 1 teaspoon vanilla extract

Instructions:

1. Preheat your oven to 350°F (175°C). Grease and flour a 9x5-inch loaf pan or line it with parchment paper for easy removal.
2. In a large mixing bowl, whisk together the all-purpose flour, granulated sugar, baking powder, baking soda, and salt until well combined.
3. Stir in the chopped fresh cranberries and orange zest until evenly distributed throughout the dry ingredients.
4. In a separate mixing bowl, whisk together the melted unsalted butter, eggs, orange juice, and vanilla extract until well combined.
5. Pour the wet ingredients into the dry ingredients and stir until just combined. Be careful not to overmix.
6. Pour the batter into the prepared loaf pan, spreading it out evenly with a spatula.
7. Bake in the preheated oven for 50-60 minutes, or until a toothpick inserted into the center comes out clean.
8. If the top of the bread starts to brown too quickly, you can tent it loosely with aluminum foil halfway through baking.
9. Once baked, remove the bread from the oven and let it cool in the pan for 10-15 minutes before transferring it to a wire rack to cool completely.
10. Once cooled, slice and serve this delicious cranberry orange bread as a delightful breakfast or snack.

11. Enjoy the moist and flavorful cranberry orange bread with a cup of coffee or tea!

This homemade cranberry orange bread is sure to be a hit with its tangy cranberries, bright orange flavor, and tender crumb. It's perfect for sharing with friends and family during the holiday season or any time you're craving a festive treat.

Rice Krispie Treats

Ingredients:

- 6 cups Rice Krispies cereal
- 1 package (about 10 ounces) marshmallows
- 3 tablespoons butter or margarine

Instructions:

1. Grease a 9x13 inch baking dish or line it with parchment paper.
2. In a large saucepan, melt the butter over low heat.
3. Add the marshmallows to the melted butter and stir until completely melted and smooth.
4. Remove the saucepan from heat and quickly stir in the Rice Krispies cereal until well coated.
5. Transfer the mixture to the prepared baking dish.
6. Use a greased spatula or wax paper to press the mixture evenly into the dish.
7. Let the treats cool completely before cutting into squares.

You can also get creative with Rice Krispie Treats by adding in extras like chocolate chips, nuts, or even shaping them into fun shapes before they cool. Enjoy!

Marble Cake

Ingredients:

- 2 cups all-purpose flour
- 1 teaspoon baking powder
- 1/2 teaspoon baking soda
- 1/4 teaspoon salt
- 1/2 cup unsalted butter, softened
- 1 cup granulated sugar
- 2 large eggs
- 1 teaspoon vanilla extract
- 1/2 cup milk
- 1/4 cup cocoa powder
- 1/4 cup hot water

Instructions:

1. Preheat your oven to 350°F (175°C). Grease and flour a 9-inch round cake pan or line it with parchment paper.
2. In a medium bowl, whisk together the flour, baking powder, baking soda, and salt. Set aside.
3. In a large mixing bowl, cream together the softened butter and sugar until light and fluffy.
4. Beat in the eggs, one at a time, then stir in the vanilla extract.
5. Gradually add the dry ingredients to the wet ingredients, alternating with the milk, beginning and ending with the dry ingredients. Mix until just combined.
6. In a small bowl, mix the cocoa powder and hot water until smooth to create the chocolate batter.
7. Pour half of the vanilla batter into the prepared cake pan. Spoon dollops of the chocolate batter on top of the vanilla batter.
8. Use a knife or skewer to swirl the chocolate batter into the vanilla batter, creating a marbled pattern.
9. Pour the remaining vanilla batter over the top and repeat the swirling process.
10. Bake in the preheated oven for 30-35 minutes, or until a toothpick inserted into the center comes out clean.

11. Allow the cake to cool in the pan for 10 minutes, then transfer it to a wire rack to cool completely before slicing and serving.

Enjoy your delicious homemade marble cake!

Baked Alaska

Ingredients:

- 1 sponge cake or genoise cake, baked and cooled (store-bought or homemade)
- 1 quart (about 1 liter) of your favorite ice cream, slightly softened
- 4 large egg whites, at room temperature
- 1/2 cup granulated sugar
- 1/2 teaspoon vanilla extract

Instructions:

1. Line a small bowl with plastic wrap, leaving some overhang. Place the softened ice cream into the bowl, pressing it down firmly and smoothing the top. Cover with the overhanging plastic wrap and freeze until firm, at least 2 hours or overnight.
2. Once the ice cream is firm, preheat your oven to 500°F (260°C). Place the cake on a baking sheet lined with parchment paper or aluminum foil.
3. Remove the ice cream from the bowl using the overhanging plastic wrap to lift it out. Invert the ice cream onto the center of the cake and remove the plastic wrap.
4. Quickly spread the meringue over the ice cream and cake, making sure to seal the edges completely.
5. Bake in the preheated oven for 3-5 minutes, or until the meringue is lightly browned. Keep a close eye on it to prevent burning.
6. Remove the Baked Alaska from the oven and serve immediately, or return it to the freezer to firm up for a few minutes before serving.
7. Slice and serve your Baked Alaska, enjoying the contrast between the warm, toasted meringue and the cold, creamy ice cream.

You can also get creative with the flavors by using different types of cake and ice cream.

Enjoy this decadent dessert!

Raspberry Chocolate Tart

Ingredients:

For the Tart Crust:

- 1 1/4 cups all-purpose flour
- 1/4 cup unsweetened cocoa powder
- 1/4 cup granulated sugar
- 1/2 cup unsalted butter, cold and cut into cubes
- 1 large egg yolk
- 2-3 tablespoons ice water

For the Chocolate Filling:

- 8 ounces semi-sweet chocolate, chopped
- 3/4 cup heavy cream
- 1 tablespoon unsalted butter

For Topping:

- Fresh raspberries
- Powdered sugar, for dusting

Instructions:

For the Tart Crust:

1. In a food processor, pulse together the flour, cocoa powder, and sugar until combined.
2. Add the cold butter cubes and pulse until the mixture resembles coarse crumbs.
3. Add the egg yolk and 2 tablespoons of ice water. Pulse until the dough starts to come together. If needed, add an additional tablespoon of ice water.

4. Turn the dough out onto a lightly floured surface and knead it briefly until it forms a smooth ball.
5. Flatten the dough into a disk, wrap it in plastic wrap, and refrigerate for at least 30 minutes.
6. Preheat your oven to 375°F (190°C). Roll out the chilled dough on a lightly floured surface into a circle slightly larger than your tart pan.
7. Carefully transfer the dough to a 9-inch tart pan with a removable bottom. Press the dough into the bottom and up the sides of the pan. Trim any excess dough.
8. Prick the bottom of the crust with a fork. Line the crust with parchment paper or aluminum foil and fill it with pie weights or dried beans.
9. Bake the crust in the preheated oven for 15 minutes. Remove the parchment paper and weights and bake for an additional 5-7 minutes, or until the crust is set and dry.
10. Remove the crust from the oven and let it cool completely.

For the Chocolate Filling:

1. Place the chopped chocolate in a heatproof bowl.
2. In a small saucepan, heat the heavy cream and butter over medium heat until it just begins to simmer.
3. Pour the hot cream mixture over the chopped chocolate and let it sit for 1-2 minutes.
4. Stir the chocolate and cream together until smooth and well combined.
5. Pour the chocolate filling into the cooled tart crust and spread it out evenly.

Assembling the Tart:

1. Arrange fresh raspberries on top of the chocolate filling.
2. Refrigerate the tart for at least 1 hour, or until the filling is set.
3. Before serving, dust the tart with powdered sugar.
4. Slice and serve chilled. Enjoy your raspberry chocolate tart!

Feel free to customize this tart by using different types of berries or adding a drizzle of raspberry sauce on top for extra flavor.

Eclairs

Ingredients:

For the Choux Pastry:

- 1/2 cup (1 stick) unsalted butter
- 1 cup water
- 1 cup all-purpose flour
- 1/4 teaspoon salt
- 4 large eggs

For the Pastry Cream:

- 2 cups whole milk
- 1/2 cup granulated sugar
- 4 large egg yolks
- 1/4 cup cornstarch
- 2 teaspoons vanilla extract

For the Chocolate Glaze:

- 4 ounces semisweet chocolate, chopped
- 1/2 cup heavy cream
- 1 tablespoon unsalted butter

Instructions:

For the Choux Pastry:

1. Preheat your oven to 400°F (200°C). Line a baking sheet with parchment paper.
2. In a medium saucepan, combine the butter and water. Bring to a boil over medium heat.

3. Once the butter is melted and the mixture is boiling, remove the saucepan from the heat.
4. Stir in the flour and salt until the mixture forms a ball of dough and pulls away from the sides of the saucepan.
5. Transfer the dough to a mixing bowl and let it cool slightly, about 5 minutes.
6. Using a hand mixer or stand mixer, beat in the eggs one at a time, mixing well after each addition, until the dough is smooth and glossy.
7. Transfer the dough to a piping bag fitted with a large round tip.
8. Pipe the dough onto the prepared baking sheet into 4-inch long strips, leaving space between each eclair.
9. Bake in the preheated oven for 25-30 minutes, or until the eclairs are golden brown and puffed up.
10. Remove the eclairs from the oven and let them cool completely on a wire rack.

For the Pastry Cream:

1. In a medium saucepan, heat the milk over medium heat until it just begins to simmer.
2. In a separate mixing bowl, whisk together the sugar, egg yolks, and cornstarch until smooth.
3. Slowly pour the hot milk into the egg mixture, whisking constantly to prevent curdling.
4. Return the mixture to the saucepan and cook over medium heat, whisking constantly, until it thickens and comes to a boil.
5. Remove the saucepan from the heat and stir in the vanilla extract.
6. Transfer the pastry cream to a clean bowl and cover the surface with plastic wrap to prevent a skin from forming. Chill in the refrigerator until cold.

For the Chocolate Glaze:

1. In a heatproof bowl, combine the chopped chocolate, heavy cream, and butter.
2. Microwave the mixture in 30-second intervals, stirring well after each interval, until the chocolate is completely melted and the glaze is smooth. Alternatively, you can melt the mixture over a double boiler.
3. Let the chocolate glaze cool slightly before using.

Assembly:

1. Once the eclairs have cooled, use a sharp knife to slice them in half horizontally.
2. Fill the bottom halves of the eclairs with the chilled pastry cream using a spoon or piping bag.
3. Replace the top halves of the eclairs.
4. Dip the top of each eclair into the chocolate glaze, letting any excess drip off.
5. Place the dipped eclairs on a wire rack to set the glaze.
6. Serve the eclairs chilled or at room temperature.

Enjoy your homemade eclairs! They're best enjoyed the same day they're made, but you can store any leftovers in the refrigerator for up to 2 days.

Orange Creamsicle Popsicles

Ingredients:

- 1 cup orange juice (freshly squeezed or store-bought)
- 1 cup plain yogurt or vanilla yogurt
- 2-3 tablespoons honey or maple syrup (adjust to taste)
- 1 teaspoon vanilla extract
- Zest of 1 orange (optional)

Instructions:

1. In a mixing bowl, whisk together the orange juice, yogurt, honey or maple syrup, vanilla extract, and orange zest (if using) until well combined.
2. Taste the mixture and adjust the sweetness level if needed by adding more honey or maple syrup.
3. Pour the mixture into popsicle molds, leaving a little space at the top for expansion.
4. Insert popsicle sticks into the molds and freeze for at least 4-6 hours, or until the popsicles are completely frozen.

5. Once the popsicles are frozen solid, remove them from the molds by running warm water over the outside of the molds for a few seconds to loosen the popsicles.
6. Serve the orange creamsicle popsicles immediately and enjoy!

You can also get creative with these popsicles by adding chunks of fresh orange or even layering them with a mixture of orange juice and vanilla yogurt for a visually appealing effect. These homemade popsicles are perfect for cooling off on a hot day and are sure to be a hit with kids and adults alike!

Chocolate Lava Cake

Ingredients:

- 4 ounces (113 grams) bittersweet or semisweet chocolate, chopped
- 1/2 cup (1 stick) unsalted butter
- 1 cup powdered sugar
- 2 large eggs
- 2 large egg yolks
- 1 teaspoon vanilla extract
- 1/4 cup all-purpose flour
- Pinch of salt
- Optional: vanilla ice cream or whipped cream, for serving
- Optional: powdered sugar or cocoa powder, for dusting

Instructions:

1. Preheat your oven to 425°F (220°C). Grease and flour four 6-ounce ramekins or custard cups. Place them on a baking sheet for easier handling.
2. In a heatproof bowl set over a saucepan of simmering water (double boiler), melt the chocolate and butter together, stirring occasionally until smooth. Remove from heat and let cool slightly.
3. In a separate mixing bowl, whisk together the powdered sugar, eggs, egg yolks, and vanilla extract until well combined.
4. Slowly pour the melted chocolate mixture into the egg mixture, whisking constantly until smooth.
5. Add the flour and salt to the chocolate mixture and gently fold until just combined. Be careful not to overmix.
6. Divide the batter evenly among the prepared ramekins, filling each about 3/4 full.
7. Bake in the preheated oven for 12-14 minutes, or until the edges are set but the centers are still soft.
8. Remove the lava cakes from the oven and let them cool in the ramekins for 1-2 minutes.
9. Carefully run a knife around the edges of each cake to loosen them from the ramekins. Invert each cake onto a serving plate.
10. Serve the chocolate lava cakes immediately, topped with vanilla ice cream or whipped cream if desired. You can also dust them with powdered sugar or cocoa powder for extra indulgence.

11. Enjoy these rich and gooey chocolate lava cakes warm, and be prepared for the delight when you cut into them and the molten chocolate center oozes out!

These chocolate lava cakes are perfect for special occasions or whenever you're craving a luxurious chocolate dessert.

www.ingramcontent.com/pod-product-compliance
Lightning Source LLC
LaVergne TN
LVHW081603060526
838201LV00054B/2050